TEXTILES OF THE SILK ROAD

Design and decorative techniques: from Far East to Europe

THE ARTISTIC TRADITIONS OF NON-EUROPEAN CULTURES

VOL. 4

POLISH INSTITUTE OF WORLD ART STUDIES

TEXTILES OF THE SILK ROAD

DESIGN AND DECORATIVE TECHNIQUES: FROM FAR EAST TO EUROPE

edited by Beata Biedrońska-Słota and Aleksandra Görlich

POLISH INSTITUTE OF WORLD ART STUDIES & TAKO PUBLISHING HOUSE
WARSAW – TORUN 2016

Proofreading: *Steve Jones*

Reviews:
Prof. Dr. Piotr Balcerowicz
Prof. Dr. Waldemar Deluga

Cover design: *Szymon Saliński*
Photos: Authors' archives

ISSN 2450-5692
ISBN 978-83-65480-23-1

The book can be ordered by mail:
Polish Institute of World Art Studies – biuro@world-art.pl
Tako Publishing House – zamowienia@tako.biz.pl

POLISH INSTITUTE OF WORLD ART STUDIES
ul. Warecka 4/6 – 10, 00-040 Warszawa
www.world-art.pl
e-mail: biuro@world-art.pl

TAKO PUBLISHING HOUSE
ul. Słowackiego 71/5, 87–100 Toruń
www.tako.biz.pl
e-mail: tako@tako.biz.pl

TEXTILES OF THE SILK ROAD
Design and decorative techniques: from Far East to Europe

Table of contents

PART TWO: CENTRAL ASIA

PART THREE: FROM CENTRAL ASIA TO NEAR EAST AND EUROPE - INFLUENCES

PART FOUR: TECHNIQUE AND TRADITION THROUGHOUT ASIA

TEXTILES OF THE SILK ROAD
Design and decorative techniques: from Far East to Europe

EDITOR'S NOTE

The Artistic Traditions of Non-European Cultures is a journal issued by the Polish Institute of World Art Studies which evolved from a publishing series in 2015 (the series was established in 2009). The journal carries studies which are the effect of individual researches, as well as articles presented at scientific conferences. The journal is published mostly in English, however, depending on the subject matter it can also be published in Spanish (or, if necessary, in other congress languages). The geographical span of the journal covers Asia, Africa, Latin America and Oceania. Responsibility for each of these regions lies with academic editors: Asia – dr. (hab.) Bogna Łakomska, Africa - prof. Aneta Pawłowska, Latin America – dr. Katarzyna Szoblik.

In addition to topics related to art, theatre as well as folk culture and the artistic life of one continent or country the editorial board shall also seek universal topics that combine the traditions of those continents and study relationships between them.

It is because the belief in the need to study various forms of artistic expression which manifest themselves in cultures of the world, both in art resulting from developed aesthetic systems and that which is an expression of ethnic, folk and non-professional creation lies at the very heart of the Institute's activity.

Prof. Jerzy Malinowski

TEXTILES OF THE SILK ROAD
Design and decorative techniques: from Far East to Europe

Aleksandra Görlich

Introduction

Silk Road is one of the most important trade routes connecting the Far East with the West. Stretched from Japan to the countries of Western Europe it also became one of the most important cultural exchange routes in history. It has been a subject of studies in various fields of research. Presented here are studies concerning textiles of the Silk Road. Fifteen articles collected in the 4th volume of *The Artistic Traditions of Non-European Cultures* were presented at the international conference *Textiles of the Silk Road. Design and Decorative Techniques: From Far East to Europe* organized by the Krakow Branch of Polish Institute of World Art Studies and the Manggha Museum of Japanese Art and Technology. The conference was held on 11–13 September 2015 at the Manggha Museum in Krakow.

In this volume almost all of the conference papers are published. They are divided into four parts reflecting geographical and technical scope of their subjects: East Asia, Central Asia, From Central Asia to Middle East and Europe – Influences, and Technique and Tradition Throughout Asia. They are presented by art historians and experts of related disciplines from Poland, Ukraine, Sweden, Germany, Italy, Turkey and Japan.

The East Asia part includes articles written by Małgorzata Martini and by Maria Cybulska and Jacek Dróżdż concerning Japanese decorative techniques, *kumihimo* and *shibori*, as used by modern artists cultivating the tradition, articles by Barbara Szewczyk, by Anna Bielak, and by Joanna Bodzek on Japanese fashion phenomena since 19th century until modern times. The first part closes with an article by Ewa Orlińska-Mianowska concerning the reception of the Orient in the 18th-century European silk industry.

In the Central Asia part one can find three articles about decorative motifs moving along the Silk Road. Marta Żuchowska describes vine and grape motifs on Chinese Silks in the 1st millennium AD, Paweł Janik tries to answer a question about Xiongnu or Kushans affiliation of the faces from Noin Ula's embroidery, and Astrid Klein presents a comparative study of Kučean clothing.

Articles devoted to influences along the western part of the Silk Road begin with Kosuke Goto describing in detail sources of ornamental celestial lotus patterns woven in silk samite. This article is followed by a paper by Maria Ludovica Rosati concerning iconographic journeys of *feng huang* bird, horseman, and Hellenistic *putto*. Articles by Beata Biedrońska-Słota and by Cemile Tuna present the way the Middle Eastern clothes influenced European fashion.

The last part of the volume consists of two articles. The first one, by Natalia Shabalina, is devoted to colour in a traditional art. The paper which closes the publication is written by Racep Karadag and concerns chemical analysis of dyes used in threads and yarns from Ottoman silk brocades.

This publication is a collection of articles presenting traditions of various designs and decorative techniques spreading through the Silk Road from Far East to Europe, their connections and the way they developed. It also presents a condition of this heritage and its role in the realm of modern fashion and textile design.

PART ONE: EAST ASIA

Małgorzata Martini
Manggha Museum of Japanese Art and Technology
Polish Institute of World Art Studies

Kumihimo: an ancient art or a present-day one? The gifts of Mrs Midori Suzuki to the Japanese art collection in Krakow

Kumihimo craft is a part of the traditional Japanese art of dyeing and braiding. The craft combined two aspects: practical and decorative. The material used for *kumihimo* is silk.

In Japan *kumihimo,* just like the other handicrafts of this country, attained a very high level of development over the ages. The beautiful *kumihimo* had been in use from the Asuka (538–710) and Nara (710–794) periods and there is a major heritage of these cultural objects. There are countless *kumihimo* bands in the Shōsō-in, the treasure house in Nara. They are attached to many ritual Buddhist objects as well as ordinary utensils, musical instruments, armour and arts of armament. They prove the highest quality of this craft. Almost all the bands were created in 8th c. and confirm that the greatest demand for *kumihimo* was among the emperor family as well as the aristocracy.

Many objects of plaited silk were kept in shintō shrines and Buddhist temples of all districts of Japan from the Heian, Kamakura and Muromachi periods. It seems that the superior features of *kumihimo* bands were consistently both the beauty and the functionality of the object from very simple patterns to gorgeously elaborated designs.

Let us begin with a short overview of the history of the Japanese art of *kumihimo,* the origin of which is as old as the human race itself. When our ancestors evolved into human beings, they began to gather food, hack down trees and invent some kind of covering for their naked bodies. They learnt the essential skill of joining various materials. From this skill grew the art of *kumihimo.* Plaited objects appeared independently in various parts of the world. This is proven by discoveries in China, Egypt, India and Peru as well as Europe. It is thought that plaiting is older than weaving.

String and braids of ingenious workmanship were made in Japan in the 7th and 8th c. They were designed not only for practical use but were also considered as objects of art, and as such they were preserved in treasuries like Shōsō-in or Hōryū-ji. It was only in Japan that braids were accompanied by an indication of their use and description of the technique. Many of the them maintain their good state of preservation due to the fact that they were kept, first of all, in buildings like temples and shrines and treasure houses.

In Japan the skill of plaiting was not limited to purely practical uses such as joining or binding but it was raised to the rank of art. The uses of *kumihimo* were diversified according to the many aspects of human life, activity and human needs connected with them. Let us name the most important:

- Armament – strings binding the various parts of armour, sword, bow and horse gear
- Garments – strings and kimono belts (*kumiobi*), head coverings
- Religious objects – strings and bands binding scrolls, ornamental elements of Buddhist temples and shintoistic shrines
- Strings and bands attached to mats, mirrors and boxes
- Toys, musical instruments – elements of costumes worn for court dance (bugaku), mask bands

Nowadays many items of *kumihimo* craft can still be found in Buddhist temples and Shintō shrines and museum of Japanese art as well.

When in the early nineties NHK, the Japanese national TV channel, broadcasted a program introducing a collection of Japanese traditional art from the National Museum in Krakow, it bore unusual fruit. Many people in Tokyo showed a deep interest in the subject, expressed in strong support for a project presented by Andrzej Wajda. He proposed the erection of a separate building, where the collection of Japanese art that is housed in Krakow would be preserved and made permanently available for the general public. Andrzej Wajda's project was successfully followed through and the opening ceremony of a new Centre of Japanese Art and Technology "Manggha" took place on 30th November 1994 (today the institution is known as the Manggha Museum of Japanese Art and Technology).

It also turned out that Mrs Midori Suzuki – one of the most eminent Japanese artists who still continue the traditional art of string braiding – watched the program shown by NHK, and she noticed that numerous swords of the Krakow Japanese collection were lacking some very important details – *kumihimo* strings.

Ill. 1.
Uchigatana sageo by Midori Suzuki, braided silk dyed with natural pigment (Japan, 1994). National Museum in Krakow, deposited with the Manggha Museum of Japanese Art and Technology; inv. number MNK VI-NN-58

Ill. 2.
Uchigatana sageo by Midori Suzuki, braided silk dyed with natural pigments (Japan, 1994). National Museum in Krakow, deposited with the Manggha Museum of Japanese Art and Technology; inv. number MNK VI-NN-57

The subtly braided silk *kumihimo* strings, formed in complicated *sageo* knots, were made for a practical purpose as well as for decoration, as was not fully understood in Krakow at that time.

Shortly before the opening of the "Manggha" Centre in 1994, Mrs Midori Suzuki arrived in Krakow and presented to the National Museum several hand-made *kumihimo* that she had made for the swords. On the opening day and its special exhibition, they became a splendid ornament for the Japanese art collection and are still kept there. They were as follows:

1. *Uchigatana sageo* (ill. 1) – a cord fastened to the *uchigatana* sword; made for a *tantō* dagger (a "short blade"- the sword worn by the samurai class of feudal Japan; with a false signature of Yasumitsu of Osafune (fl. 1394–1425), 19th c.)[1]
2. *Uchigatana sageo* (ill. 2) – a cord fastened to the *uchigatana* sword made for the *wakizashi* sword (worn by the samurai class in feudal Japan; signed

[1] Inventory numbers: sword with scabbard: MNK VI-6431/1-2; *uchigatana sageo*: MNK VI-NN-58.

Ill. 3.
Tachi no o by Midori Suzuki, braided silk dyed with natural pigments, brocade (Japan, 1994). National Museum in Krakow, deposited with the Manggha Museum of Japanese Art and Technology; inv. number MNK VI-NN-55

Ill. 4.
Tachi no o by Midori Suzuki, braided silk dyed with natural pigments, brocade (Japan, 1994). National Museum in Krakow, deposited with the Manggha Museum of Japanese Art and Technology; inv. number MNK VI-NN-56

Ill. 5. *Bantō kumihimo* by Midori Suzuki, braided silk dyed with natural pigments (Japan, late 20th century). National Museum in Krakow, deposited with the Manggha Museum of Japanese Art and Technology; inv. number MNK VI-NN-70

Fujiwara Yukinaga; Takada school, Bungo province; blade 17th c. It came from the Feliks Jasieński collection)[2]

3. *Tachi no o* (ill. 3) – a *sageo* cord fastened to the *tachi* sword made for the *katana* sword mounted as a *tachi* (the sword signed Kanemoto, Seki school, Mino province; blade Tenshō period (1573–1592), scabbard 18–19th c.; from the Feliks Jasieński collection)[3]
4. *Tachi no o* (ill. 4) – a plaited band for tying the *sageo* cord fastened to the *tachi* sword made for the *katana* sword mounted as a *tachi* (the sword signed Etchu no Kami Masatoshi, from Mishima / Kyoto school; Shōho (1644–48))[4]

---

[2] Inventory numbers: sword with scabbard: MNK VI-6384/1-2; *uchigatana sageo*: MNK VI-NN-57.

[3] Inventory numbers: sword with scabbard: MNK VI-6381/1-2; *tachi no o*: MNK VI-NN-55.

[4] Inventory numbers: sword with scabbard: MNK VI-6410/1-2; *tachi no o*: MNK VI-NN-56.

Mrs Midori Suzuki has been involved in *kumihimo* plaiting for many years. Now she holds the title of *Kodai kumihimo no shokunin* – "Master in the ancient craft of *kumihimo*". Her efforts, endeavour and persistence command respect and admiration for her tenacity. She learned the mastery of plaiting through a comprehensive study of history of Japanese handicrafts, for which she worked extremely hard, especially with regard to bands attached to swords and tied into special knots – *sageo* – and their history, designs, types of weaves, splices and other technical details became her favourite subject of research.

Additionally, for about six years she has learnt natural ways of dyeing, mastering traditional dyeing and discovering new technical possibilities for putting them into practice. For example, as for Japanese madder dyeing, she walks alone through an inscrutable domaine, picking the necessary herbs for dyeing depicted in ancient recipes. Preoccupied with the passion, she brings the beauty of the colour to the light of day. Braiding *kumihimo* bands, she has made friends all over the world. The fact that she works by herself and she has been successful in many walks of life is very moving in itself – and this is a priceless experience.

Since her first visit, Mrs Suzuki has already visited Krakow several times. She donated another valuable gift to the Krakow Japanese collection – a *bantō kumihimo*[5] (ill. 5). It is a band used as the head of a Buddhist flag. Mrs Suzuki used both special colours and braiding based on old methods, maintaining five traditional colours for this kind of old flag: white, orange, red, dark blue and yellow. In her oeuvre she used the method known as *sazanami gumi – ni-jō-jiku ikken gumi* – paired-strand single-unit braiding consisting of two parallel strands crossed in single-unit braiding manner in which a strand crosses over a second strand, then under a third strand, and then over a fourth strand after which the process is repeated.

During all her visits to Krakow we had a chance to enjoy her works, as well as her methods of braiding *kumihimo* strings both in a traditional and fairly modern way for a variety of bands, belts, ties, and shawls. Due to these presentations, some of the secrets concerning the technique and a symbolic meaning of the strings were partly revealed. She often underlined that Krakow's special cultural atmosphere and natural environment was extremely inspiring for her work.

Now in Poland Mrs Suzuki even has students who, thanks to her, had the opportunity to learn some rules regarding this traditional Japanese craft and make *kumihimo* on their own. The best example is Mr Janusz Lukaszczyk from Czerwionka Leszczyny – a city near Katowice – who had been deeply interested in Japanese art and crafts first for years and was trying to establish a Japanese blacksmith's shop and now, following instructions given by Mrs Suzuki, plaits *kumihimo* as well.

---

[5] Inventory number MNK VI-NN-70.

BIBLIOGRAPHY

Alber–Dzieduszycka–Martini–Romanowicz 1994 = Alber Zofia Maria, Dzieduszycka Maria, Martini Małgorzata, Romanowicz Beata, *Japanese Art in the National Museum in Krakow*, Krakow: National Museum in Krakow, Kyoto-Krakow Foundation Andrzej Wajda & Krystyna Zachwatowicz, 1994.

Dzieduszycka Maria, Kobielski Stanisław, *Uzbrojenie dawnej Japonii* (Armament of Ancient Japan), series: *Małe katalogi zabytków wybranych*, vol. 5, Kraków: Muzeum Narodowe w Krakowie, 1974.

Görlich 2015 = Görlich Aleksandra, *Wielowątkowe piękno. Techniki dekoracyjne tkanin japońskich* (A Beauty of Many Weaves. Japanese Textile Design Techniques), Kraków: Muzeum Sztuki i Techniki Japońskiej Manggha, 2015.

Król 2014 = Król Anna (ed.), *Arcydzieła sztuki japońskiej w kolekcjach polskich. Masterpieces of Japanese Art in Polish Collections*. Bilingual version (Polish-English). Kraków: Manggha Museum of Japanese Art and Technology, 2014.

Suzuki 1999 = Suzuki Midori, Kumihimo, *japońska sztuka wyplatania taśm*. Kumihimo. *Japanese Art of Braiding Bands. Bilingual* (Polish–English), introduction by Beata Romanowicz, Krakow: Muzeum Narodowe w Krakowie, 1999.

Barbara Szewczyk

"How the kimono released women from corsets" – Japonism in fashion at the turn of the 19th and 20th centuries

I would like to discuss Japonism in women's fashion on the turn of 19th and 20th centuries and to prove that the Japanese kimono had a great influence on the whole of 20th century Western fashion.

European women's fashion in the second half of the 19th century was stiff, and had a clear formalised construct. For centuries, women had been forced to wear corsets, which squeezed them tight. Sometimes this led to the deformation of the ribs, which could even puncture the organs and cause internal bleeding and death.

Almost in every decade of the 19th century, women wore special structures designed to emphasise their backside and hips. Dresses consisted of many layers. They were stiff, heavy, uncomfortable, sewn to size and closely fitted to the woman's figure.

In the 1860s, the crinoline was in fashion. It was a skirt in the shape of a bell, built on a rack made of flexible metal tape which was invented in 1851. Thanks to this discovery the rack was light and could be built in larger sizes, for example 3 meters in diameter. In the 1870s and 80s, the bustle came into fashion. The bustle was a skirt with a padded backside. For two years (between 1878–80) the princess dress was fashionable – a tight dress, without any racks (although with a corset of course) which revealed genuine feminine shapes for the first time in hundreds of years.

At the end of the 19th century, the S-shape dress dominated fashion. This new style of corset pushed the breasts up and the bottom down. The S-shape was taken from the Art Nouveau style, which was very popular in architecture and design and was inspired by nature. In architecture and fashion, one could observe wavy shapes which resembled the meandering shoots of plants, or textures which looked like the surface of leaves.

Ill. 1. "S-shape dress", illustration by Barbara Szewczyk, inspired by vintage fashion journal

Ill. 2. "Kimono", illustration by Barbara Szewczyk, inspired by Japanese woodblock print

Eastern clothes differ from Western in their form. They look completely different even before wearing. When one looks at a Japanese kimono which hangs on the traditional bamboo rack, it has the shape of a rectangle. But it looks quite different when worn due to the special method of draping and tying it. This is a completely different way of thinking about clothing.

For several hundred years, Japan isolated itself from the rest of the world for reasons of safety. However, in 1854 Commodore Matthew C. Perry from the United States came to Japanese shores and forced the Japanese authorities to reopen trade and diplomatic contacts. The treaty ensured the security of American whale ship castaways. Soon a few European countries signed similar treaties with the Japanese.

Then Japanese products started to appear in Europe and America, thanks to international exhibitions and artistically ambitious boutiques. Only then did the Western world start to distinguish Japan from China and marvelled at Japanese products.

Japanese design was completely different from European. It was elegant, tasteful, without exaggerated ornamentation. Paintings and woodblock prints showed quite a different way of thinking about two-dimensional art and this delighted the Western world. They brought woodblock prints, ceramics, painted screens, furniture, lacquer cases as well as clothing and textiles. Europeans started to wear kimonos as home wear. Artists in particular loved to paint portraits of their wives and muses dressed in these new informal clothes, which coincided with the first women's campaigns to be released from corsets and for a simplification of clothing. This was the result of a new lifestyle. Women were gradually starting to take up jobs, gaining an educating and travelling (and this was thanks to the development of the steam engine and trains). Western women were inspired by the Japanese kimono in terms of creating a new style for themselves.

Ill. 3. "Kimono style S-shape dress", illustration by Barbara Szewczyk, inspired by vintage fashion journal

However, in 19th century fashion, references to the kimono were still only decorative. Dresses sometimes had blouses with crossing flaps, wide sashes or were decorated with popular Japanese motifs – for example, irises or chrysanthemums or even Japanese traditional family crests called *kamon*. Sometimes dresses were sewn from Japanese textiles with kimono-style long sleeves. If those were domestic dresses, the women could wear their corsets a bit looser.

The approach to clothing had started to change in those days. Kimonos were also used as domestic clothes. They could have special strings for tying back the long sleeves. Alternatively, they could be stylised coats.

The Japanese had noticed that the Western world was very interested in their products and design so they had started to produce things especially for the western market. Sometimes those articles were a specific mix of Western and Eastern styles. Many Japanese traveled to Europe, for example because of international fairs. They made some research there and monitored closely what the Europeans liked. They would then send certain products to Europe – for example, home dresses or fans with Japanese elements like wood print style figures or chrysanthemum baskets, which are originally Japanese flowers, but could be expressed in a European style.

People in the times of Art Nouveau claimed that the construction of their clothes was something new, a distinct shape, a different way of thinking, whereas in reality the only visible difference was in the ornamentation. The figure looked a little different, but it was hardly a revolution. This would come around the year 1910.

At the beginning of the 20th century, Europeans wore the kimono differently than the Japanese. They wore it untied, rather like a coat. This flat, loose and wide costume influenced all 20th century fashion.

The European fascination with the Japanese was manifested in different aspects of art. At the end of the 19th century, the art of posters had developed as well as magazine illustration. Both these branches were inspired by Japanese paintings. For the first time in Western history, artists started to use flat blocks of colour without shading or light. They used a clear outline and a plain background, marking only a few elements of the landscape behind the portrayed figure. In the beginning of the 20th century in Europe, illustrations replaced prints in magazines. Japanese-style pictures had promoted more and more Japanese stylised fashion.

At the turn of the centuries, suffragettes and doctors were looking for a new form of clothing which could be more loose, comfortable and healthy. They proposed a reformed loose dress without a waistline, but these were not accepted by society because they were not deemed to be pretty enough.

We can say that the revolution was brought about by designers like Paul Poiret, who proposed a completely innovative cut inspired exactly by a loosely worn kimono. He said that he had discovered this form thanks to his intense search for new forms of beauty.

For the first time in hundreds of years the centre of gravity of a dress was pushed from the waist to the shoulders. The waistline disappeared to be replaced by a completely opposite shape. Poiret designed loose dresses that widened midway across the figure – a total inversion of what women had worn for centuries.

Paul Poiret was inspired by the East, Arabian clothing and of course the Japanese. Interest in the Middle East grew with the launch of the Orient Express railway as well as the translation and publication of the book "One Thousand and One Nights".

There was also a very popular Russian ballet group from Diagiliev who put on very beautiful shows with spectacular oriental style costumes and became an

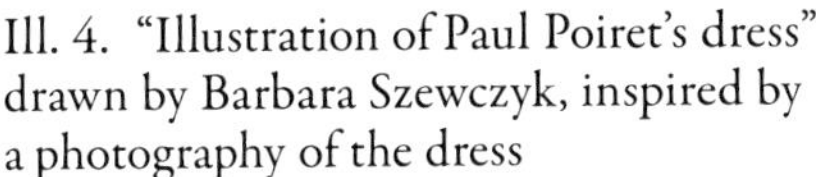

Ill. 4. "Illustration of Paul Poiret's dress" drawn by Barbara Szewczyk, inspired by a photography of the dress

Ill. 5. "Illustration of Paul Poiret's dress from 1910" drawn by Barbara Szewczyk, inspired by a photography of the dress

inspiration for women, tailors and designers. Japanese products became popular again because of the Russo-Japanese war of 1904–05. Dresses often took the shape of an open kimono or were sewn from kimono fabric.

The Delphos gown designed by Mariano Fortuny was made from one piece of fabric without any seam, with patent pleats. Inspirited by an ancient tunic and clipped together with Venetian glass beads, it was supposed to flow over the female body and reveal its natural shapes. Very often it was worn along with a kimono as a coat.

Fortuny was interested in Japanese dyeing techniques. Previously, he had used wooden blocks for dyeing. However, inspirited by the Japanese template dyeing technique, he wrapped the blocks and started to dye textiles according to the screen printing method.

So we can see that the Japanese kimono had a great influence on the modernisation of European women's fashion. The kimono gave Western women comfort and forever changed the way we would think about clothes.

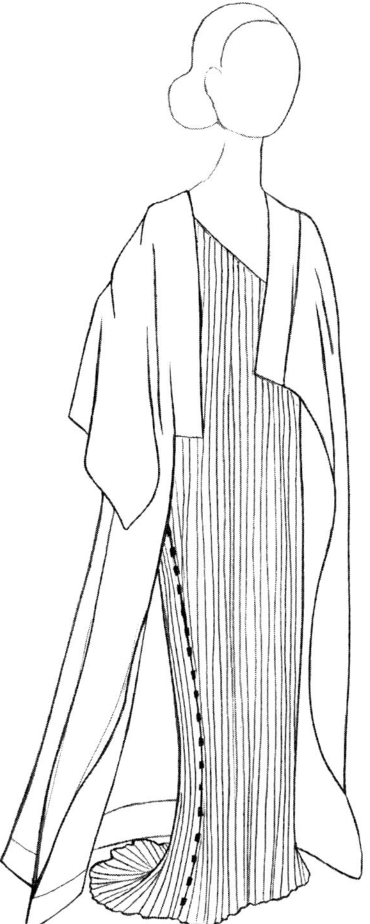

Ill. 5. "Illustration of Mariano Fortuny's dress" drawn by Barbara Szewczyk, inspired by a photography of the dress

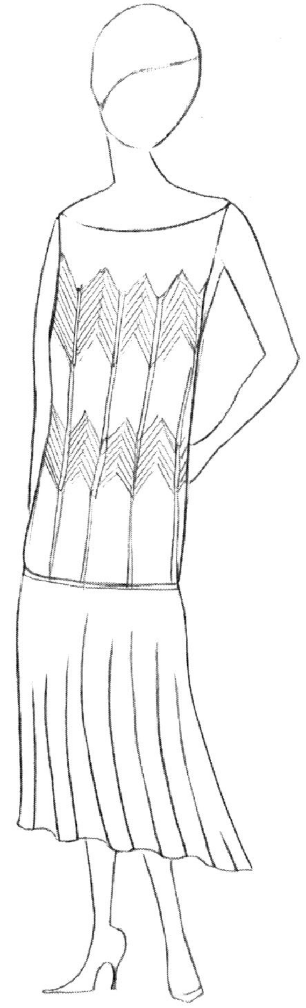

Ill. 6. "Illustration of Paul Poiret's dress from 1924" drawn by Barbara Szewczyk, inspired by a photography of the dress

Bibliography

Fukai 2002 = Fukai Akiko (ed.), *Moda. Historia mody od XVIII do XX wieku* (Fashion. A History from the 18th to the 20th Century), Kioto: Kyoto Costume Institute, 2002.

Kunai 1996 = Kunai Jun I., *Japonism in fashion*, Tokyo: Kyoto Costume Institute, 1996.

Wichmann 1999 = Wichmann Siegfried and Whittall Mary, *Japonisme: The Japanese Influence on Western Art Since1858*, London: Thames & Hudson Publishers, 1999.

Zaborowska 2004 = Zaborowska Barbara, *Kimono. Jego dzieje i miejsce w kulturze japońskiej* (Kimono. Its History and Place in the Japanese Culture), Warszawa: Wydawnictwo TRIO, 2004.

Anna Bielak
Manggha Museum of Japanese Art and Technology

The kimono as a fashion phenomenon in modern Japan and beyond

The kimono with its characteristic tailoring is one of the symbols of Japanese culture. After opening to the West, during the Meiji period (1868–1912), Western clothes grew in popularity and the kimono became a garment of choice rather than an obligation and showed an affection to tradition.[1] During that time different styles were sometimes mixed but generally the Japanese increasingly took to western clothes. Although kimonos were still worn (mostly by women), the lowest point in the popularity of the kimono happened during the first two decades of the post-war period.[2] Over time, the kimono came back as an occasional garment, worn rarely for special occasions or more often by people connected to Japanese traditional arts.[3] The form that is now often seen as the one and only true traditional form of kimono comes mostly from the Edo samurai class garment. Presently, the kimono style has become standarised, with many rules concerning the kimono, obi, accessories, way of wearing, occasions etc. Proper *kitsuke* (donning a kimono) requires practice and knowledge. As Lisa Dalby states: "contemporary kimono are marked by their limitations, not their potential".[4]

But this is only one face of the kimono world. On the threshold of the 21st century it became also a worldwide fashion phenomena. Mixing styles, breaking canons and combining Japanese tradition with contemporary design – on the one hand, the kimono with its fashionable appeal returned as a second-hand item and became

---

1 *Victoria and Albert Museum* (2015).
2 Yamanaka (2009: 39–40).
3 Okazaki (2015: 9).
4 Dalby (2001: 126).

closer to everyday life while, on the other hand, it entered the world of modern styles and the great world of fashion.

Such kimono reinvention was interpreted by Terry Satsuki Milhaupt as a longing for a slower and more traditional style of life which could be noticed in Japanese society with its fast-changing and ever-growing bubble economy of the 1980s and its end in the 1990s.[5] A trend for second-hand kimonos began to gain popularity and kimono fans started searching for new inspirations and pretexts for wearing the kimono more often than only official occasions and Japanese holidays.[6]

In the year 2000 in Tokyo Ginbura kimono meetings – *Kimono de Ginza* – were reactivated. To this day, anybody who looks for a pretext to wear a kimono and meet other kimono fans is welcome there. 10 years later a similar initiative called *Kimono de Jack* started up in Kyoto which, after some time found followers among kimono fans – at first in the United Kingdom, then in different countries around the world.[7]

A continuation of this idea are the Krakow Kimono Meetings – *Kimono de Krak (Kimono de Jack Krakow)*. During such meetings participants refer not only to Japanese tradition but also to their own kimono style and modern trends, so unconventional elements appear in their kimono sets, adding a personal touch or, for example, hats or gloves during a cold day.[8]

This trend, noticeable at the beginning of 21st century, of modernising the kimono and the attempt to look at the kimono with a more "playful attitude" (*asobi gokoro*),[9] more as everyday fashion than ceremonial wear, Yasuko Suzuki calls the "kimono boom". In 2004 she became an editor-in-chief of *Nanao Magazine,* which was supposed to meet the expectations of modern women interested in the kimono, who want to derive some inspiration from tradition, are not afraid to use the kimono of their mothers, grandmothers and from flea markets, but at the same time strive to keep up with the latest fashion trends.[10] Among the many articles presenting the new face of the kimono, readers can find advice on creating their own obi belts from modern textiles as well as for non-standard collars (for example, handmade ones with cross stitching)[11], sets breaking the usual canons (like wearing a sweater under a kimono during winter) or a fresh look at traditional elements (for example, looking at a wool kimono as an everyday pair of jeans)[12].

---

5 Milhaupt (2014: 9).

6 Suzuki (2011: 7).

7 Milhaupt (2014: 246).

8 "Krak" comes from the name of the Krakow city, Kimono de Krak became an official part of Kimono de Jack in 2016; KimonoTEKA (2016).

9 Milhaupt (2014: 9).

10 Suzuki (2011: 7).

11 Onodera (2011: 42–44).

12 Saito (2011: 62–65).

Ill. 1.
Kimono de Jack meeting in Kyoto (April 2016). Each person with their own kimono style. Photo: Akagi Mihiro

Ill. 2.
Kimono de Jack Krakow (Kimono de Krak) meeting in Krakow (September 2016). Participants wearing kimono with Polish traditional elements (red bead necklaces and scarfs).
Photo: Łukasz Bielak

Ill. 3.
A kimono fan during kimono shopping in Nagoya, wearing a modern kimono coordination with Western shoes and bag.
Photo: Anna Bielak

Ill. 4. Akagi Mihiro (initiator of Kimono de Jack) in denim kimono designed by Jōtarō Saitō. Photo: Anna Bielak

Ill. 5. Kaonn's obi bets made of French fabrics. Photo: Anna Bielak

In 2014 in Krakow we had the chance to meet a person who is a living example of the reinvention of the kimono by modernising its form. Takeo Kitsunai tries to popularise wearing the traditionally non-formal narrow obi belt *hanhaba obi* on formal occasions. By this kimono becomes more friendly to a modern women, easier to wear and giving possibility of having fun with tying obi belt in many different ways. She said: "My goal is to popularise *kitsuke* that is comfortable and neat, and at the same time shows not only the beauty of the dress but also of the person who wears it".[13]

The non-traditional way of looking at the cotton *yukata* is also an interesting trend. Traditionally, it was treated separately from the kimono, as informal attire, mainly worn while relaxing and during summer festivals. The informality that comes with the *yukata* allows the creation of even more non-standard sets. What is more, according to "Nanao" magazine's editors, thanks to the unconventional setting of the *nagoya obi* (more formal than the one used normally for the *yukata*)

[13] Presentation "A Passion for Kimono" by Takeo Kitsunai and her students, Manggha Museum of Japanese Art and Technology, Krakow, 25.10.2014.

and the *juban* (underkimono) with the *yukata*, one can widen its usage and, for example, go to a restaurant. Like many fashion innovations, this too has not won acceptance in the more traditional sectors of kimono society, but one cannot deny such a trend in the modern kimono world.[14]

For the same reason *yukata* patterns are especially interesting objects connecting the traditional world with fashion. It is very easy to find *yukata* that are a background for modern patterns. This trend became so natural that a large Japanese clothing producer joined in and designed special *yukata* and obi sets, creating original patterns inspired, for example, by the works of Japanese artists (like Yumeji Takehisa).[15]

Creating original trendy patterns applies to the kimono too. It is enough to mention Jōtarō Saitō, Iroca or Anyan to realize the existence of such strong and colourful modern designs. Jōtarō Saitō is the third generation of his kimono-dyeing family but he is also the only kimono designer that appears regularly at Tokyo Fashion Week. His works are described as a mix between traditional quality, fresh sensibility and futuristic themes.[16]

Iroca is a one-man brand of Narutoshi Ishikawa. He is a *yukata* and kimono designer creating original designs with a slightly dark touch, with jellyfish, mythical creatures and fantasy forest elements.[17] On the works of Anyan (a graphic, textile and product designer) we can find cute animals, characters with a humorous touch and the influence of French literature as well as European folk patterns.[18] Foreign inspirations appear also in the works of Yoshioka Kaori. Under her own brand, Kaonn, she both creates her own modern designs and makes *obi* and other kimono related items from French fabrics.[19] All these are far from traditional Japanese motifs, but thanks to such innovative approaches they can combine very well with the kimono form.

A very special example of treating the kimono as a picture are the kimonos made by Itchiku Kubota. The beautiful landscapes on his kimono are not meant to be worn but to become a piece of art on the border of tradition (restoring the forgotten technique of *tsujigahana*), fashion and painting.[20]

When talking about Japanese fashion of any kind, it is difficult not to mention Tokyo's Harajuku, where the streets are famous for unusual subcultures and fashion experiments. There you can meet a whole range of inspirations.[21] For some,

---

14 Suzuki (2011: 79–83).
15 Uniqlo (2015).
16 Okazaki (2015: 66–71).
17 Okazaki (2015: 76–79).
18 Okazaki (2015: 82–83).
19 Kimono research trip, Kyoto, 13.04 – 05.05.2016.
20 The Kubota Collection (2015).
21 Adamowicz (2015).

the kimono has only been a starting point for the imagination and the connection to traditional form is only symbolic, for others, the kimono remained a traditional outfit but in a very non-standard, modern style.[22]

One such extremely non-traditional trend, with followers not only in Japan but also around the world, is the *Kimono Hime* style, where *hime* is the Japanese world for princess. This style looks like a condensation of contrasts between the traditional form of the kimono and elements breaking its standards. It seems like an invitation to feel like a fashion designer who treats the kimono as a basis for artistic research. Abstract hair styles, kimonos as short skirts, high-heeled shoes, obi knotted at the front, in the style of Japanese courtesans with many bows, necklaces or hats – none of these becomes a surprise when we see the kimono princess. Interestingly, at the same time you need only take one look to notice the kimono shape in this playful stylisation. In Japan you can also find a special paper magazines called *Furisode Hime*[23] and *Kimono Princess* (Kimono Hime)[24], which already has an international on-line version called *Go Hime*.[25]

Kimono inspirations outreaching traditional garments are a phenomenon that is quite easy to notice among many fashion designers and artists. In the wide world of fashion, the kimono inspires on many levels. One of those would be the new lease of life for the kimono set, as can be seen, for example, in Wafrica, created by designer Serge Mouangue and Odashō.[26] They presented kimonos and obi made of textiles with African designs but worn as a whole in a traditional form. Among other kimono inspirations we can find characteristic kimono shapes (for example, as in Alexander McQueen works[27]), using the whole kimono in a new abstract setting (Natasha Ygel[28]), recycling fragments of kimonos in shoes (Hetty Rose) and other clothes (Julie Richards[29]) or using traditional kimono fabric techniques in fashion (Amy Nguyen and her *shibori*[30] and Pagong's Hawaiian shirts decorated according to the traditional Japanese *yūzen* technique[31]).

It is quite obvious that globalisation, wide-spread Internet access, social networks, international trade and Japanese pop-culture had a great influence on spreading both conventional and unconventional modes of kimono dress. Paradoxically,

---

22 Tokyo Fashion (2015).
23 Kimono research trip, Kyoto, 13.04 – 05.05.2016.
24 Kimono Princess (2010: 4–51).
25 Go Hime (2015).
26 Okazaki (2015: 86–87).
27 Okazaki (2015: 139).
28 Okazaki (2015: 146–147).
29 Okazaki (2015: 152–153).
30 Okazaki (2015: 143).
31 Okazaki (2015: 154–157).

Ill. 6.
Kimono related magazines: *Nanao, Kimono Hime* and *Furisode Kimono.* Photo: Anna Bielak

Ill. 7.
Shoes made of traditional textile for obi created by the Ohba family (an artisan family from Nishijin district in Kyoto). Photo: Anna Bielak

modernity made it possible not only to present kimono tradition all around the world but also to swap the latest trends and kimono textiles themselves. Accordingly, fashion trends in the kimono world and kimono elements in the fashion world coexist and combine to bring newer and fresher ideas, projects and inspirations not only among kimono fans but also artists, designers and craftsmen in Japan and beyond.

BIBLIOGRAPHY

Dalby 2001 = Liza Dalby, Kimono. Fashioning Culture, London: Vintage, 2001.

Kimono Princess 2010 = *Kimono Princess* (Kimono Hime), 10 (2010): 4–51.

Milhaupt 2014 = Terry Satsuki Milhaupt, *Kimono. A Modern History*, London: Reaktion Books Ltd, 2014.

Okazaki 2015 = Manami Okazaki, *Kimono Now*, Prestel Verlag, Munich – London – New York.

Onodera 2011 = Hiromi Onodera, "Free and Easy – Your Very Own Nagoya Obi", in: *The New Kimono*, Yasuko Suzuki (ed.), Tokyo – New York – London: Kodansha International, 2011.

Saito 2011 = Megumi Saito, "A Wool Kimono Is Like a Pair of Jeans", in: *The New Kimono*, Yasuko Suzuki (ed.), Tokyo – New York – London: Kodansha International, 2011.

Suzuki 2011 = Yasuko Suzuki (ed.), *The New Kimono*, Yasuko Suzuki (ed.), Tokyo – New York – London: Kodansha International, 2011.

Yamanaka 2009 = Norio Yamanaka, *The Book of Kimono*, Tokyo – New York – London: Kodansha International, 2009: 39–40.

Internet

Adamowicz 2015 = Klaudia Adamowicz, "Harajuku – historia w pigułce" (Harajuku – Short History), in: *Japonia-Online*, 8.10.2015: http://japonia-online.pl/article/500 (entry: 30.11.2015). *Go Hime*: http://www.saiya-chan-com.pcxtmp.nl/gohime/ (entry: 30.11.2015).

KimonoTEKA: http://kimonoteka.pl/kimono-de-jack-krakow/ (entry: 30.09.2016).

The Kubota Collection: http://www.thekubotacollection.com/en (entry: 30.11.2015).

Tokyo Fashion: http://tokyofashion.com/tag/kimono/ (entry: 30.11.2015).

Uniqlo: http://www.uniqlo.com/us/product/women-yumeji-takehisa-yukata-157929.html (entry: 30.11.2015).

Victoria and Albert Museum: http://www.vam.ac.uk/content/articles/h/a-history-of-the-kimono/ (entry: 30.11.2015).

Practical

Kimono research trip, Kyoto, 13.04–05.05.2016.

Presentation *A Passion for Kimono* by Takeo Kitsunai and her students, Manggha Museum of Japanese Art and Technology, Krakow, 25.10.2014.

Maria Cybulska, Tomasz Dróżdż
Lodz University of Technology

Traditional Japanese shibori and contemporary textile design

Introduction

Japanese traditional textiles are manufactured according to a large variety of methods, like weaving, embroidery and dyeing. Weaving includes many different techniques: from the simplest *hira-ori* (plain weave) gauze *monsha*, *rinzu* (which is the type that we call damask), to most splendid *karaori* (patterned and brocaded silk) and *nishiki* made from gold threads. However, the most interesting are different, very sophisticated, refined and often labour-intensive methods of patterned dyeing, printing and painting, like katazome, yuzen, kasuri, surihaku and shibori. Most interestingly and intriguingly, all these methods are often applied together in one cloth. In Ill. 1, one can see coupons of Japanese silk, usually around 36 centimetres wide and 12 meters long, each designed to sew a single kimono. Regardless of how complicated the weaving process is, if it is simple cotton fabric in plain weave or luxury silk brocaded or patterned, it often undergoes further manipulation and decorating by embroidery, painting, printing or dyeing techniques.

Tie dye and shibori

Shibori, which is the main subject of the paper, belongs to a wide variety of methods of patterning textiles in the dying process, called patterned resist dyeing. They all involve applying different methods and solutions, protecting some areas of cloth or yarns against the penetration of dyes, which we call resists. The process can be repeated many times with the use of different dyes and different resists, resulting, after removing the protecting material, in colourful patterned cloth. Resist dyeing includes well known methods like batik, ikat and a very wide group called tie-dyeing. All these methods have their origins in Eastern cultures: in Indonesia, China India and, of course, Japan. We should mention that in these cultures patterned dyeing is treated as a form of art. Sometimes the process of textile designing and manufacturing is a part of spiritual and social life. The cloth on which patterned dyeing is performed is just like a canvas is to a painter. We can see it in many examples of Java sarongs and Indian saris but first and foremost in the kimono.[1]

Europeans had always focused on woven silks which were the most prestigious. With the exception of a few decades of the 18th century, dyed and printed fabrics were usually a cheaper substitute for patterned woven, while the East has always shown more concern for resist dyeing. Shibori was known in Japan at least 1300 years ago where it came from China, along with the Chinese style of dress. The name of the technique was adopted from the Chinese word *xie,* mentioned in a historical document in the 5th century.[2] It became popular among dyers and artists from the 1980s, when Japanese textiles – thanks to the successes of Japanese fashion designers – aroused great interest among contemporary fibre artists.

Traditional shibori techniques

Shibori is a traditional Japanese textile technique. It involves refining fabrics through very complex and time consuming handwork. Certain areas on the cloth are reserved from dyeing by binding dots, tying, knotting or stitching.

The shibori family includes numerous resist processes. There are about 15 different variations of the technique. The most popular are kanoko, miura, kumo, nui, itajime and arashi. Usually one person is specialised in one particular technique, and most often several people work together on a single work.

The basic technique of Shibori, *kanoko,* involves binding sections of cloth and securing by tying it with thread to achieve the desired pattern built from small circular shapes (ill. 1 – top on left). After designing the pattern of the cloth, the artisan must draw thousands of tiny dots which follow the pattern. Each dot must then be bound by thread to separate that piece from others. Sometimes up to 150,000 binding dots are needed to finish a short-sleeve kimono. When the fabric is completely bound, the material must be bleached to remove stains. The fabric is then dyed; however the dye does not penetrate the knots. When the dyed material is dry, the binding threads are removed. When the textile is untied there is a pattern of dyed and undyed areas. This process can be repeated many times to produce patterns

[1] Wrońska Friend (1990: 93).
[2] Feng, Wada (2014: 1).

Ill. 1.
Coupons of silk for a traditional Japanese kimono.
Photos: Maria Cybulska

of various colours. The cloth with completed bindings is called *ashirome*. Depending on the size of the cloth or number of bindings required, it can take more than one year to complete the shirome process.[3]

As it can be seen in the photograph in ill. 2, the resists not only protect the cloth but also give a very characteristic texture, manipulating the cloth into a three dimensional object.

Kanoko is the most labour-intensive shibori technique. That is why on many Japanese silks, the kanoko shibori pattern is only a printed imitation. For a better effect, the cloth can be embossed, just like on the one side of the *obi* presented in ill. 1 (top right). Imitations can be made with the use of stencils, hand painting or even weaving. Faux shibori can be also found among the works of famous fashion designers such as Issey Miyake who, in his 2008 collection of "nagagi" coats that were very Japanese in style, used a woven imitation of shibori.[4] A good example is the hand woven black and white wool with irregular square motif reinterpreting *kanoko*.[5]

Miura is a technique that involves looping and binding. A hook and needle are used to pinch sections of cloth, which are then wrapped around with thread. Since there are no knots in *miura*, this kind of shibori is very easy to bind and unbind and therefore is very often used. It results in a softer watermark design. *Miura* has been often used in combination with other techniques. In ill. 1 (centre left) we can see it coupled with *kanoko*, embroidery and *surihaku* (stencil).

Kumo shibori is a pleated and bound resist. This technique involves pleating sections of the cloth very finely and evenly. Then the cloth is bound in very close

---

[3] ABOUT "SHIBORI".

[4] Issey Miyake, Etlob Tep.

[5] Issey Miyake Hand Woven Faux Shibori Wool Coat, https://a.1stdibscdn.com/archivesE/jewelry/upload/49/521/20thX_49_1283208287_1.jpg.

Ill. 2.
At the top: *kanoko shibori*, silk, (left) imitation of *kanoko* (right); in the centre: *miura shibori* (left), *kumo shibori* (right); at the bottom: Catherine Ellis 2010, fragment, digital jacquard shibori, cotton (left), Tomasz Dróżdż 2014, silk fragment painted and dyed with rust and *arashi shibori* (right). Photos: Maria Cybulska

sections. The result is a very specific spider-like design. This technique is very precise and easy to produce. *Kumo* appears frequently in the *ukiyo-e* wood-block prints of the Edo period (1603–1868). Now there are many modifications of *kumo* varying by the amount of binding used to resist the fabric, which is pulled and gathered into hornlike units. The result is a pattern of radiating lines against the reserved white ground or reverse *kumo shibori* also uses different objects as the resists. The cloth is wrapped around these objects and held in place with thread.

Nui is a technique that simply involves stitching the cloth and pulling the threads tight to gather the fabric. Wooden dowels are used to pull the thread very tight and to secure it in place when dying. This technique allows a variety of patterns to be achieved that are determined by the type of stitch, whether or not the cloth is folded, and the arrangement of the stitches – straight, curved, parallel, and so on. Stitching in rows of straight lines results in a wood grain pattern called *mokume*.

A version of *nui shibori* is the so-called woven shibori where a number of shibori wefts, as they are called, are inserted while weaving the basic fabric. After weaving they are pulled tightly, to create a resist. Finally, the work is dyed. After dyeing, the shibori threads are removed and the full colour pattern is revealed. This technique is very popular among American artists, fascinated both by hand weaving and dyeing, although these works are woven on an industrial jacquard loom (ill. 1 bottom on left).

Itajime shibori is a shape resistant technique where the fabric is folded and clamped with two pieces of wood. The fabric is folded several times at differing tensions to create different effects. Wood is traditionally used but modern interpretations use clamps and pieces of plastic. Sometimes the fabric is merely folded and wrapped with threads or other material. This is very popular among young artists and designers and students, because it is quick and easy, and is used especially in home textiles but also in garment. A good example are cloths designed and manufactured by the young American designer Amy Nguyen. By using silk organza and itajime shibori and stitching, she managed to achieve both simplicity and complexity. "Each work may appear simple, yet involves many processes and layers involving technical skill and innovative ideas. Cloth is stitched and folded, coloured with dyes, cut or torn apart, and stitched back together. A final design is chosen, patterned or draped and then finished carefully. The inside of each piece matters as much as the outside. It is not a singularly dimensional piece."[6]

The last technique, Arashi, is also known as pole wrapping shibori. Arashi involves twisting, wrapping and binding the cloth around poles made from wood or copper. The fabric is twisted and wrapped diagonally around the pole, then bound and pushed along. This always gives a diagonal pattern that is easily recognisable. Contemporary textile artists have adapted the original process using a shorter plastic pipe and by manually turning the pipe or winding the threads by hand.[7]

Arashi is very popular because it can create interesting 3D effects and sculptural qualities and today is often used even without dyes just to give a cloth an interesting texture.

The Modern Shibori

Although in Japan the kimono is no longer as common a costume as it used to be, we can still find some stunning examples combining the work of fashion designers and master dyers. A wonderful example of a contemporary shibori is the Tokuseu Hitome furisode kimono from the collection of Metropolitan Museum of Art in New York.[8] Thanks to his mastery, the dyer managed to create a continuous pattern that precisely passes through the middle seam and between the main part of kimono and the sleeves, combing all the parts into one whole. This beautiful

6 Amy Ngueyn homepage.
7 Wada, Rice, Barton (1999: 295).
8 http://www.metmuseum.org/collection/the-collection-online/search/79595.

design exhibits extreme craftsmanship – the piece was tied and dyed eleven times with 3,600 knots per square "shaku" [30 × 30 cm].[9]

Shibori is applied not only in traditional Japanese garments but also in fashion by contemporary fashion designers, such as Yohji Yamamoto. "With my eyes turned to the past, I walk backwards into the future" – this famous quotation sums up his philosophy of fashion that references both his Japanese heritage and innovations in fashion. From his first collection in 1977, he has sought new ways of dressing the body form and, together with other Japanese designers, has changed world trends by incorporating the aesthetic philosophy of Japanese costume with its minimalist sculptural form of draping the body – multi-layering, loose-fitting, looking like untailored clothes and with the emphasis on the material. Yamamoto, who never wanted to be called a "Japanese" designer, introduced Japanese tradition and heritage not only in the form of cloth but also by using shibori and yuzen fabrics in his works.[10] For the 1994 autumn-winter and 1995 spring-summer collections, Yamamoto reached deeper into his cultural heritage to produce a collection that was spiritually and technically Japanese, as was apparent both in the form of the clothing and the beautiful handmade shibori fabrics produced by skilled Japanese artisans (ill. 3). "Maybe I will be the last designer who cares strongly about 'Made in Japan'. If I stop, maybe young designers cannot afford to do business that way. It costs a lot; a Japanese man's hand has become the most expensive in the world. So it's my duty – not duty – it's my desire to protect these small, traditional Japanese techniques. I use almost all family factories. The most important thing is to keep going, otherwise it will disappear".[11]

The word shibori comes from *shiboru*, "to wring, squeeze, press." Although shibori is used to name a particular group of resist-dyed textiles, the root of the word emphasises the action performed on the cloth, the process of manipulating the fabric. As mentioned before, shibori gives a flat fabric a three-dimensional form. This potential of the material, also called the memory or shape memory of the cloth, is the most inspiring feature for contemporary designers, as Issey Miyake, for whom, as he said, a research on new methods of making cloth and development of new materials, combining craftsmanship and new technology, is very interesting.

"PLEATS PLEASE ISSEY MIYAKE", a famous fashion project, is a good example where both these aspects came together. Change of form is supported by the change of material by folding, twisting, and wringing. Derived from the kimono idea that the material properties shape the clothing as well as the clothing function developed a new fashion perspective. Thermoplastic polyester was used

---

[9] Recent Acquisitions, A Selection: 1997–1998. (1998: 76–78).

[10] Yohji Yamamoto (2011: 14).

[11] Yohji Yamamoto, The Talks (2011).

as the main material processed by folding or pleating and using heat and pressure. Textures produced by crimps easily change and move, which makes sewing the cloth after processing difficult. Therefore, the cloth is sewn prior to processing; and sometimes it is up to 3 times larger than the final size. Afterward, the pleats are processed.[12]

Simple folds such as accordion, box and crinkle pleats are machine-made using a fully automated process. Pleating machines use a roller system to feed the fabric, sandwiched between two sheets of paper, through the machine in a continuous length Instead of the needles used in shibori where a blunt blade traps the paper and cloth layers onto a heated metal, pushing the fabric up into a pleat. However, fully automated processes cannot undertake many of the more complex folding patterns.[13]

Wrinkle P fabric (ill. 5), developed by the Inoue Company, is produced half manually, by randomly stuffing polyester fabric into a small container and heating it under high temperature in order to permanently set the pleats. It resembles the effect of *miura shibori* with irregular binds and an overshaped 3D structure.[14]

Ill. 3. Yohji Yamamoto, Woman's Kimono Coat and Sleeveless Dress. Collection of LACMA. © 2015.Digital Image Museum Associates/LACMA/Art Resource NY/Scala, Florence*

[12] Kitamura (2012).

[13] Philpott (2012: 53–73).

[14] McCarty, McQuaid (1998: 26).

* Yamamoto, Yohji (b. 1943): Woman's Kimono Coat and Sleeveless Digitale (1) Dress, Spring/Summer 1995. Los Angeles (CA), Los Angeles County Museum of Art (LACMA). 1) Coat: Tie-dyed (shibori) silk;.2) Dress: Silk..1) Coat centre back length: 64 in. (162.56 cm);.2) Dress centre back length: 46 in. (116.84 cm). Los Angeles County Museum of Art, Costume Council Fund (AC1996.158.4.1). © 2015. Digital Image Museum Associates/LACMA/Art Resource NY/Scala, Florence.

In Ill. 4 we can see the cloth sewn from the most traditional shibori-like method from all Miyake works presented in the paper. Just like the other Pleat Please clothing, it was sewn before processing. The fabric represents a polyester heat set shibori which was then embroidered. We can see the fabric was pleated not by using moulds or random folds but by stitching with threads which created an accurate pattern and were pulled before applying the heat. This method resulted in a random 3D effect incorporated to the structure regularly arranged by stitching. It can be called *nui shibori*.

One of the artists and designers working for Miyake is Norma Starszakovna. For Starszakovna the most important word in designing is innovation. She has developed and used innovative printing techniques and experimented with different materials. The fabric we can see in the Ill. 5 was developed by her for the Miyake Studio and is called crushed shibori. The silk organza is stitched with thread which is then pulled and the cloth is printed with vinyl, latex or another rubber-like printing media. After applying some amount of tension this layer of latex is torn along the lines of prior stitches. It gives the cloth a dynamic 3D look resembling alligator leather.

These ideas open a new perspective on the traditional Japanese textile industry. Shibori inspired textiles are made manly from thermoplastic polyester for its heat-setting capabilities, and are thus sometimes called thermoplastic shibori characterised by a 3-dimensional structure, applied not only in clothing but also in home furnishings. Many manufactures of these textiles are large factories, although there are also small workshops which have made kimono for many generations.[15]

One such company is Urase Company. The Harmony (ill. 5), known from the cover of the MOMA catalogue of contemporary Japanese textiles exhibition, uses heat to transfer a dark blue colour onto an already wrinkled yellow fabric. As a static piece of cloth, it simply looks wrinkled; however, when the wrinkles are pulled apart, as if to straighten out the cloth, the yellow interior colour is revealed.[16]

Suzusan uses shibori methods to create decorative fabrics. Many of their fabrics have been used in collections by designers such as Junya Watanabe, Calvin Klein, Issey Miyake and Yohji Yamamoto. The roots of Suzusan are in the Japanese town of Arimatsu, where the Murase family has been working with the traditional shibori technique for over 100 years. "Do not just keep the tradition. Create it." Under this motto, Hiroyuki Murase, designer at Suzusan attempts to give the technique a more contemporary relevance. Suzusan produces not only for famous fashion

---

[15] McCarty, McQuaid (2002: 12).

[16] McCarty, McQuaid (2002: 26).

Ill. 4. Issey Miyake, blouse, pleated thermoplastic polyester. Photo: Maria Cybulska

Ill. 5.
At the top: detail of the pleated polyester from ill. 4 (on left), traces of the threads applied before thermal setting of the fabric (right); in the centre: Blizzard and Accordion fabrics, Inoue Pleats Company; at the bottom: Harmony, Urase Company (left), Norma Starszakovna, crushed shibori, organza and thermoplastic print (right).
Photos: Maria Cybulska

designer but also offers its own, more traditional shibori fashion accessories as well as home products such as lamps, placing traditional Japanese craft in a modern, European context.[17]

Inoue Pleats Company is known because of the Miyake Pleats Please collection. Presented in Ill. 5, the Blizzard and Accordion are machine pleated. The previously mentioned Wrinkle P and Crystal S are manufactured half manually. They represent machine pleated and manually compressed thermoplastic polyester.[18]

This way the polyester we do not like that much, shows quite different face when coupled with shibori technique and attracts many contemporary fibre artists, not only in Japan.

Yuh Okano is an American designer. She works with polyester and silk by applying shibori to create three-dimensional forms or highly textured expressive surfaces, sometimes using metal disks or glass beads. Her polyester textile sculpture installation entitled "Epidermis: Ocean" incorporated shibori fabric into objects resembling corals and sea animals in a fantasy underwater environment. One of her methods for obtaining such effects is the use of beads made from urea resin, which is resistant to very high temperatures. The beads are wrapped in very fine polyester cloth and bonded with rubber bands. She dyes cloth, and then repeats the process with another dye to add a second colour in the convex places. The material is then heated to fix the fabric form and the beads are removed. Yuh Okano uses shibori for her art and for fashion accessories such as scarfs and bags.[19]

Liivi Leppik from Estonia is another designer working with thermoplastic shibori. She produces curtains, lamps and other home furnishings. Grassy Garden is a heat-set polyester shibori that creates a form resembling spring grass. In her work we can recognise kumo and arashi shibori ideas.[20]

Born in Korea, Jeung-Hwa Park uses a contemporary adaptation of the shibori technique in combination with felting and knitting. The knitted fabrics are bound, tied, stitched, crimped, or folded to prevent certain areas from absorbing colour or to give them a 3D shape. Combining traditional technique and modern technology, hand craft and machine knitting, Park brings new sculptural and textural properties to traditional knitted goods. Park shows that textural, innovative 3D shibori effect is possible not only on modern fibre but also when applied to traditional materials like wool and silk.[21]

[17] Fumihiro (2014: 148–149).
[18] McCarty, McQuaid (2002: 26, 74–78).
[19] Okano (2014: 309–313).
[20] Liivi Leppik Homepage.
[21] Searle (2008: 26–31).

The work of Ivanaga Yasuko entitled "A Gift from Sea-Air X"[22], presented at the "Fiber Futures: Pioneers of Japanese Textile Art", exhibition is made from silk and wire, with the use of *kumo* and *arashi shibori*. The exhibited works show the most interesting features of the new Shibori. Textiles are becoming multi-dimensional and sculptural; artists employ an astonishing fusion of forms and materials, from silk, wool, cotton, hemp, paper to metal and synthetic fibres. Using a combination of traditional methods of decorating the textiles and the latest textile technologies, they create works that combine the past and present as well as being innovative and beautiful. They show how to take advantage of the rich Japanese tradition to give the future of textiles a new direction.[23]

Conclusions

This paper shows the potential of traditional shibori in creating new modern textiles. Shibori is very popular among young artists and designers. Some of my students are also fascinated by this and other resist dying techniques. However when one tries to find Polish artists or designers working with shibori, there are very few examples that are interesting or innovating. Why? Shibori is really quite specific and one might describe it as a spiritual or somehow paradoxical technique. It is labour-intensive and risky, because with no long-term experience you can never be sure of the outcome of the design. However, the results can sometimes amaze and what we could think of as an "error" may in fact lead to some very interesting results because the patterns and shapes are at the same time very free and, on the other hand, need to be constructed very carefully. Furthermore, one needs imagination and also a knowledge of traditional and innovative materials and technologies. Finally, it is necessary to be humble and patient and ready to work hard with one's own hands. This is a real challenge for people in this era.

Bibliography

Earle, Watanabe 2011 = Joe Earle, Hiroko Watanabe, *Fiber Futures: Pioneers of Japanese Textile Art*, Japan Society, New York, 2011.

Feng, Wada 2014 = Zhao Feng, Yoshiko Iwamoto Wada, "Introduction", in: *Resist Dye On The Silk Road. Shibori, Clamp Resist and Ikat*, Proceedings for the 9th International Shibori Symposium at the China National Silk Museum, October 31st–November 4th, Hangzhou 2014: 1.

Fumihiro 2014 = Murase Fumihiro, "Suzusan", in: *Resist Dye On The Silk Road. Shibori, Clamp Resist and Ikat*, Proceedings for the 9th International Shibori Symposium at the China National Silk Museum. October 31st–November 4th, Hangzhou 2014: 148–149.

---

22 http://redtextilia.org/wp/wp-content/uploads/2014/03/Fiber-future-2.jpg.

23 Earle, Watanabe (2011).

Kitamura 2012 = Midori Kitamura, *Pleats Please Issey Miyake*, Taschen, 2012.
McCarty, McQuaid 1998 = Cara McCarty, Matilda McQuaid, *Structure And Surface: Contemporary Japanese Textiles*, The Museum of Modern Art, New York 2002: 12–78.
Okano 2014 = Yuh Okano, "Epidermis. Textiles in Art vs Art in Textiles", in: Resist Dye On The Silk Road. Shibori, Clamp Resist and Ikat, Proceedings for the 9th International Shibori Symposium at the China National Silk Museum, October 31st–November 4th, Hangzhou 2014: 309–313.
Philpott 2012 = Rachel PHILPOTT, "Crafting innovation: the intersection of craft and technology in the production of contemporary textiles", *Craft Research*, 3(1), 2012: 53–73.
Salazar 2011 = *Yohji Yamamoto*, Ligaya Salazar (ed.), exhibition cat., Victoria & Albert Museum, London 2011.
Searle 2008 = Karen Searle, *Knitting Art: 150 Innovative Works from 18 Contemporary Artists*, Voyageur Press, Minneapolis 2008: 26–31.
Wada, Rice, Barton 1999 = Yoshiko Iwamoto Wada, Mary Kellogg Rice, Jane Barton. *Shibori: The Inventive Art of Japanese Shaped Resist Dyeing: Tradition, Techniques, Innovation*, Kodansha International, 1999: 295.
Wrońska Friend 1990 = Maria Wrońska-Friend, "Techniki ochronne (rezerważowe) w farbiarstwie tekstylnym. Systematyka i rys historyczny" (Resist techniques in the textile dyeing. Classification and historical outline), *Kwartalnik Historii Kultury Materialnej* no. 1–2, 1990: 93–145.
Yamamoto 2011 = Yohji Yamamoto: "People Have Started Wasting Fashion", The Talks, August 31, 2011. Available from: http://the-talks.com/interviews/yohji-yamamoto/ (accessed December 20, 2015).

INTERNET

"Recent Acquisitions, A Selection: 1997–1998", *The Metropolitan Museum of Art Bulletin*, v. 56, no. 2, New York 1998: 76–78. Available from: http://resources.metmuseum.org/resources/metpublications/pdf/Recent_Acquisitions_A_Selection_1997_1998_The_Metropolitan_Museum_of_Art_Bulletin_v_56_no2_Fall_1998.pdf (entry: 12.05.2015).
"Passion for Fashion, Kerry Taylor Auctions 8th December 2015", Jamm Design Ltd, 2015: 58. Available from: http://issuu.com/jammdesign/docs/kt_8th_dec_2015/40 (entry: 20.11.2015).
Yuh Okano homepage, http://textilesyuh.com (entry: 1.08.2015).
Liivi Leppik homepage, http://www.visioontekstiil.com (entry: 12.08.2015).
Amy Ngueyn homepage, http://www.amynguyentextiles.com/ (entry: 31.08.2015).
ABOUT "SHIBORI", http://bunzaburo.com/en/ (entry: 2102.2015).
Issey Miyake, Etlob Tep, http://isseymiyake.co.jp/ELTTOB_TEP/en/semba/2008/08/spring_summer_2008_new_in_augu_1.html (entry: 22.11.2015).

Joanna Bodzek
Stokholm

To [mend] *

A reflection on the Lee Edelkoort anti-fashion manifesto, the Kimono Reconstruction Project – my personal vision on how mended clothes can mean "style" in the future and how this is connected with the Boro textiles of Japan

The Kimono Reconstruction Project is my brain child born out of an impulse that comes from a love of clothes, influenced by Butoh and Wabi Sabi aesthetics that speak to me in a language of inspiration. Although this may appear to be a work about Japan, it is in fact born out of a love of clothes, texture, textiles, dyes... and the future. However, it also reflects my loss of interest in fashion as such. Fashion like the Titanic, heavy and proud, unable to change its course, remains unaware of the world around, subsequently losing its power and appeal.

Fashion is dead, trend forecaster Lee Edelkoort declared, describing the fashion industry as "a ridiculous and pathetic parody of what it has been". Lidewij Edelkoort, one of the world's most influential fashion forecasters, used her annual presentation at Design Indaba to fire a broadside at the industry. She told Dezeen magazine, "This is the end of fashion as we know it". Edelkoort said, her interest in fashion had now been replaced by an interest in clothes, since fashion has lost touch with what is going on in the world and what people want. "Fashion is insular and is placing itself outside society, which is a very dangerous step".

Boro is clothing that was worn by peasants, merchants or artisans in Japan from the Edo period up to the early Showa (17th–early 19th century) and became a popular collector's piece among textile lovers and art collectors. Boro was born out of the forgotten values of 'mottainai' or 'too good to waste' – an idea dangerously lacking in the modern consumer lifestyle...

KI-MONO Reconstruction Projects aim is to combine Western and Eastern cultural aspects, visual traditions, roots, preferences and ideals of beauty while creating a new space beyond East and West, a platform for both cultures to meet. Kimono Reconstruction is also a tribute to imperfection, to the unfinished, to the non-persistent, the mysterious and the reused. There are reused collaborations, ideas and the extensive common textile stocks from the participants. Almost nothing in the project is newly purchased...

The idea of making a kimono from valuable rags made by women in Sweden and Poland occurred to me long before I knew about Boro or even much about Japanese culture, for that matter.

I wanted the project to reuse old textiles and embed personal memories within them, textiles that I and other collaborators has collected over the years. A decision was made not to buy anything new during the project. When I needed to buy fabrics and materials I would buy anything vintage that had previously been handmade specially by women to use at home, like tea towels, bed linen, tablecloth etc. I wanted these fabrics to bear witness to thousands of hours of artistic work not always seen as such.

Long before I knew about the existence of the patched textiles of Japan, Kimono Reconstruction Project was to be a recycling project in any possible way.

The inspiration that I later found in Boro, not only in actual textiles but also in their history, the way they came about as well as the reason behind them being made at all, tells me that the Boro textiles and their aesthetic values and stories are strongly related to the future of our clothes.

I wanted to see those rare scraps, that are not anymore to be found in their places of their origin, Aomori prefecture, due to recent interest in them by the world collectors.

In search for Boro I traveled to Tokyo equipped with my camera to visit Amuse Museum, the museum displaying a collection of Japanese ethnologist Chuzaburo Tanaka born in Aomori prefecture who, during 50 years of collecting work, acquired approximately 30,000 pieces of Boro clothing and artefacts accompanied by detailed explanations for each piece.

Boro come from the poorest and the most extreme areas of Japan where even cotton thread welding was a luxury. In the frozen landscape of the northern climate, most of the people who lived there had to be self-sufficient for food, shelter and clothing. To buy anything with money was not really possible in this area. The transformation from "something that people just wrapped around their bodies" to the clothes of today, took placed only recently.

In the cold and snowy mountains of Aomori with its bitterly cold climate even the smallest rugs were not wasted since clothes were more important than food. A family could own about 1000 scraps says Mr. Tanaka in one of the comments to his own collection.

Boro was born out of necessity, repetitive patching and repairs of one and the same textile sometimes for several decades. Once the piece of cloth was made, it would be maintained throughout the owner's lifetime, or longer. The use of patterned stitched into the fabric, known as Hishizashi, would adorn a garment and make it much stronger.

It was not uncommon, for a person, during one lifetime to only own one Kimono, one futon and one futon cover, mended over and over again over the years, patched, repaired and reused. The women in the house would collect the scraps of fabric and they became cherished as a most valuable possession because then they were used to repair the family kimono, futon, bedding and Donja – a very large, and extremely heavy sleeping coat – alongside with numerous other items repaired or created out of this hemp scraps. Seeing the Donja at the Amuse Museum touched me in a very special way. I could almost see this Japanese family, parents and children. They would sleep naked together inside a Donja, wrapped in layer upon layer of Boro scraps and wadding where shared body heat would protect them from freezing in this cold winter night. I could see them sleeping in this kimono-like garment, putting their arms into the huge sleeves to prevent the Dinja from sliding off...

Patched diapers would hang on strings and colourful Tabi socks, entirely made of patches, would be placed beside the futon covered with bodoko (a multi purpose bed sheet). Certainly, the Boro carry in its stitches the story of the family, the ancestors, their status and their economy.

Boro and the future

Interestingly Mr. Tanaka himself draws a parallel to fashion by reflecting on one of the greatest fashion icons Coco Chanel and the fact that "when she died in 1971 (she) left only two suits hanging in her wardrobe at the Hotel Ritz (where she lived). Throughout her lifelong career this work clothes were probably her most important possession, no evening dress nothing fancy just two suits she would alter as needed and that was enough to get by. Knowing what's really important and necessary for oneself that is a real wealth, that's what Boro teaches us," he remarks.

In her interview for Dezeen Magazine, Lee Edelkoort also says, “Finally a new breed of consumer has emerged, ” arguing that fashion does not cater to them. “The consumers of today and tomorrow are going to choose for themselves, creating and designing their own wardrobes, ” she writes. “They will share clothes amongst each other since ownership doesn’t mean a thing anymore. They will rent clothes, lend clothes, transform clothes and find clothes on the streets.”

Looking at Boro aesthetics I would like to suggest that this is perhaps how, what we call STYLE and ELEGANCE, can evolve in the future, leading to permanent change in how we look at durability and the quality of things including our clothes, as well as a change in the perception of the visual qualities of “mending”.

Many of you can agree that repaired and reused clothes and items do not have a natural place among what we regard as being “elegant and stylish” in the world today. At least, not real signs of wear and tear but only fashionable faux mending-look-alike effects are accepted and sought after in fashion, interior design, textile design etc.

Fashion and the ones who follow it, usually change because of a trend, and trends sometimes derive from necessity and important World events like the Second World War fashion, for example; then the visual appearance, what we regard as style, can change dramatically. Difficult as it is to imagine in current times when slick glamorous images are being thrown out from every advert, it is enough to look around to see that we are approaching a similar reality of scarcity of resources. Overusing our world and nature has created a “throw-away” culture leading us closer and closer to a stop-and-rethink moment.

I love unexpected effects and defects and the beauty that lies hidden in many discarded objects such as those present in kimonos made for the Kimono Reconstruction Project. The kimono we have pieced and patched together out of our collected stock of yarns of garments, of the ideas and collective wealth of our skills, is the best witness to above theories.

Boro uses everything and wastes nothing. The ‘beauty of practicality’ or ‘Yuyo-no-bi’ is a concept we may adopt for the future, just like in the case of Boro out of necessity in order to take care of the planet and natural resources. This will certainly change the visual appearance of clothes; perhaps patches and mending, reusing and repairing will come here to stay not only as a fashion gimmick but to truly awaken an appreciation of the unfinished, imperfect, the increased value in the old and the broken, the cracks and crevices so perfectly present in the Japanese Wabi aesthetics but today somewhat lacking even in the country of its origin. Inspired by the story of appreciation for nature, life and beauty despite the scarcity, I find in the Japanese Boro a possible solution for a problem our consumer culture is facing right now and will do so even more in future: Waste.

Ill. 1. Winter undergarment, Boro was born out of forgotten values of 'mottainai' or 'too good to waste. This soft and stretch MERIYASU undergarment was warm and soft to the skin. Those who could not afford new made their own undergarments from old kimono and rugs with cotton wadding stuffed between the layers. Chūzaburō Tanaka collection. Photo: Joanna Bodzek

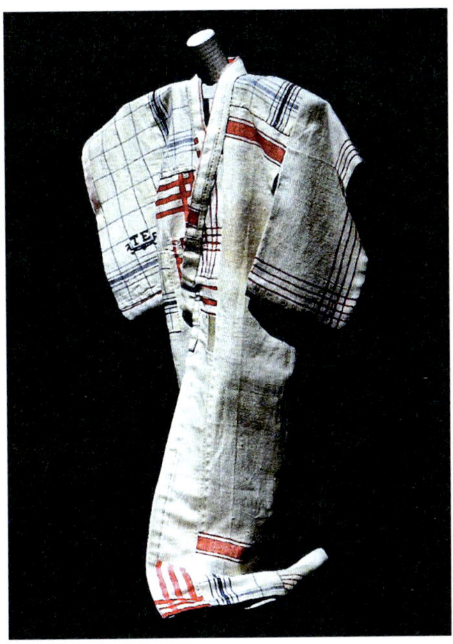

Ill. 2. The Kimono Reconstruction Kimono made out of Polish and Swedish Tea towels. The idea of making a kimono from valuable rags made by women in Sweden and Poland occurred to me long before I knew about Boro, but I recall similar thoughts and ideas while working on the above kimono that I later discovered in Boro. Joanna Bodzek collection. Photo: Joanna Bodzek

Ill. 3. Textile scraps from Aomori Prefecture, Japan. A family could own a 1000 pieces of textile scraps usually made of hemp with cotton threads woven into it to make it warmer, as cotton was not possible to grow in the mountain areas and so it was a luxury for the villagers. Amuse Museum, Tokyo. Photo: Joanna Bodzek

Ill. 4.
Boro Futon Cover. A strikingly graphic, hand-pieced work of art. Using sewing techniques to make the garment stronger. Soft parts of rice straw called SHIBI were used as a substitute for expensive cotton wadding, in case of meager rice harvest dried grass was stuffed into their home span futon covers like this. Amuse Museum, Tokyo. Photo: Joanna Bodzek

Ill. 5.
Futon and Futon cover details of mending and stitches. Repetitive patching and repairs of one and the same bedding or futon lasted sometimes for several decades. Worn out spots on the futon covers were repaired with white hemp cloth. Chūzaburō Tanaka collection. Photo: Joanna Bodzek

Ill. 6.
Donja and bedding. Donja is a very large and heavy sleeping coat, large enough for the whole family to sleep in during cold winter nights. As Chūzaburō Tanaka describes it: "The winters in the northern prefectures are severe and could and could take many lives if one was not prepared. In poorest households during pre-war days this threat was even greater, we needed our Donjas to be as thick as possible to keep us warm. Spreading straw on the floor, lying on a Boro carpet we could finally go to sleep by wearing this thick Donja" Photo: Joanna Bodzek

Ill. 7.
Adult diapers. "As machines become more and more efficient and perfect, so it will become clear that imperfection is the greatness of man." (Ernst Fischer) Image: adult diapers from Chūzaburō Tanaka collection, from the Aomori Prefecture, Japan. They belonged once to his grandmother, she readied this diaper from old towels and cotton scraps for the time when she would became bed-ridden. The beautiful composition and delicacy of of colours make them today to rare, unintentional art. Today such objects are sold for thousands of dollars as they became, sought after by the collectors, textile art pieces. Photo: Joanna Bodzek

Ill. 8.
Bodoko. The Bodoko is a 'lifecloth'. On a daily basis, it was a bed sheet. However, it was also used when giving birth. Women would hang from ropes fastened to the ceiling and kneel on the bodoko. Layers of rags worn by ancestors would be the first thing the baby would touch. "Every childbirth was accompanied by the infinite circle of life and death. The newborn baby delivered on the BODO receives unspoken blessings from it. A universal understanding on the profound meaning of BODO is: "You are not and will never be alone, look at this BODO that holds you, you are protected among the all embracing numbers of descending family bonds, you are now officially part of us, Wellcome!" writes Chūzaburō Tanaka in the story of this Bodoko. Chūzaburō Tanaka's collection at the Amuse Museum. Photo: Joanna Bodzek

Ill. 9. Boro Jacket and detail. The Amuse Museum, Tokyo. Boro uses everything and wastes nothing. The 'beauty of practicality' or 'Yuyo-no-bi' is a concept all but forgotten in today's world. Photo: Joanna Bodzek

Ill. 10. Ki-mono Reconstruction, half scale kimono made of collected scraps of textiles, printed samples. Fabric was left outdoor wrapped in metal for several weeks to be dyed with natural rust dye. Joanna Bodzek collection. Photo: Joanna Bodzek

Bibliography

Internet

http://www.dezeen.com/2015/03/01/li-edelkoort-end-of-fashion-as-we-know-it-design-indaba-2015/ (entry: 10.09.2016).

http://www.amusemuseum.com (entry: 10.09.2016).

http://www.trendtablet.com/ (entry: 10.09.2016).

http://kimonoreconstruction.joannabodzek.com/ (entry: 10.09.2016).

Practical:

The facts about Boro are taken from Chūzaburō Tanaka's comments on his collection.

Photos from Amuse Museum and Kimono Reconstruction, copyright Joanna Bodzek.

[mend] to make (something broken, worn, torn, or otherwise damaged) whole, sound, or usable by repairing.

Thanks to: Japanstiftelsen and Helge Ax: son Johnsons stiftelse.

Ewa Orlińska-Mianowska
National Museum in Warsaw
Polish Institute of World Art Studies

Reception of the Orient in the eighteenth-century European silk industry

Oriental textiles were an inspiration for the European silk industry in the eighteenth century. This period was extremely fruitful in terms of the development of silk patterns and weaving techniques. Changes in patterns and evolution of their style remained closely related to changes in style in other areas of art.[1] References to the Orient often reached much deeper than copying popular pattern books with Chinoiserie and incorporating them into the composition of silk designs. In the first half of the eighteenth century they also included the enrichment of European weaving techniques with new ways of patterning taken from Eastern textiles and transferring the motifs and their composition (ills. 3 i 4).[2]

In the patterns of some silks of that period one can even recognise the effects of the ascetic in relation to the Rococo Japanese aesthetics. They appeared in the designs of these silks in the same way as miniature motifs[3] – fans, frames, furniture – on Japanese kimonos. Such geometric elements distributed among the stems of floral branches appeared in the late seventeenth century shortly before the first phase of the bizarre – referred to as exotic in the years (1707–1710).[4]

In the patterns of silks from the 1690, wavy diagonal rhythms appeared, just like in landscapes from the *Rimpa school* (ill. 2).[5] The irrationality of patterns of silks

---

[1] Thornton (1965); N. Rothstein (1984: 214–215, 223–225, nr cat. N3, N4, N11, N12).
[2] Leclercq (2001: 139–141).
[3] Miller (2007: 155), Slomann (1955: 153–154, 158–159).
[4] Thornton (1958: 269, fig. 3); P. Thornton (1965: 98).
[5] Miller (2007: 155,159, Fig. 100); Hayao (1988: 55–56).

called *bizarre* manifests itself in the confusion of plant and architectural forms and in reversed proportions (ill. 1).[6]

Dress and textiles

In addition to the patterns, the form of Eastern costume also affected the European fashion of the period. At the end of the seventeenth century, dressing-gowns in both women's and men's versions were very popular in Europe.[7] They appear in the inventories in seventeenth-century Dutch archives under the name *japonsche rocken* next to other objects of Eastern origin. Unfortunately, their examples have not been preserved.

The collection of the National Museum in Warsaw contains a piece of a man's garment – a sleeve with a cuff (ill. 5). This sleeve is sewn from European brocaded silk with fancy oriental patterns from the first half of the eighteenth century. It is difficult to accurately determine its place of manufacturing. This is perhaps part of a home garment or stage costume in the Oriental style.[8]

The oldest records on imported garments come from 1641. It is known that at the end of the seventeenth century they were imported from the Coromandel coast – where chintz were produced for the Japanese market. They were called *sarasy* and were designated to sew kimono *kosode* for the Japanese market. Engelbert Kaempfer (1651–1716)[9], the physician of the director of the company in Nagasaki, sent a vivid description of the change of clothing patterns at the end of the seventeenth century. He admired them during an audience with the shogun Tokugawa Tsunayoshi (1646–1709). The director of the company received from the shogun a robe from soft silks with unusual designs.[10] The beauty and comfort of the garments was the reason why *Japons rocken* Japanese robes became popular in the Netherlands.[11]

In the Dutch museums similar garments have survived from the Edo period. Archives indicate that 123 items of this type of clothing were imported from the shogunat in 1692.[12] These comfortable clothes from the Netherlands became popular throughout Europe. In England it was called the *Banyan* (from a caste of Indian merchants), and in France they were known as *Indienne* – Indian style (ill. 6).[13] A wide dressing

6 Ackermann (2000), E. Orlińska-Mianowska (2001: 197–211).
7 Alieen Ribeiro (2001: 26, 27, 75).
8 This piece of silk inv. No SZT 320 was not published before.
9 Miller (2007: 161), Peck (2013: 5 Fig. 3); Fukai (1994: 2).
10 Bodart- Bailey (1999: 400).
11 Orsi Landini (2007: 197).
12 Fukai (1994: 2).
13 Peck (2013: 5).

Ill. 1.
A fragment of bizarre silk with abstractive patterns of architectural forms; inv. no SZT 116 a,b. Photo: National Museum in Warsaw

gown, with an open cut front, lined with fabric in different colours, modelled on Eastern kaftans – we can admire the various versions that appeared in representational eighteenth-century portraits. To emphasise their oriental character, they were sewn from imported fabrics: Indian printed cotton, Chinese silks and European bizarre silks, silks with lace patterns and brocades with three-dimensional patterns.

The banyan dressing-gown with a similar cut (also called a morning gown, *robe de chambre* or nightgown) in versions for men and women were not the only garment inspired by the Orient (ill. 6). The straight cut of Japanese clothing, with its folded

Ill. 2.
A fragment of bizarre silk with rhythmically intertwining tendrils with fancy forms half vegetable half animal; inv. no. SZT 67.
Photo: Ligier Piotr / National Museum in Warsaw

Ill. 3. A fragment of lace pattern silk; graphic effect and composition similar to shibori; inv. no. SZT 73.
Photo: National Museum in Warsaw

Ill. 4. Large lacy pattern referring to the Persian and Ottoman fabrics. Combined in this chasuble with Turkish fabric in the same period. In this yellow French woven-lace motifs - refer to the sas leaves, characteristic of designs of Turkish fabric; inv. no. 1335. Photo: Piotr Ligier / National Museum in Warsaw

Ill. 5.
This fragment of sleeve is sewn from European brocaded silk with fancy oriental patterns from the first half of the eighteenth century. It is difficult to accurately determine the place of manufacturing. This is perhaps part of home garment or stage costume in the Oriental style; inv. no. SZT 320. Photo: National Museum in Warsaw

Ill. 6.
Embroidered dress and morning gown; inv. no. SZT 2931 a/b and SZT 2954

final form, was also the prototype for the court dress, which appeared in the late seventeenth century.[14]

A robe called the mantua was a comfortable alternative to a tight dress with a corset and separate skirts that were commonly worn. A mantua had a loose fit, broad, reaching the elbow sleeves, and a long train.[15] The overskirt was typically drawn back over the hips to expose the petticoat beneath. In the earliest mantuas, the long trained skirt was allowed to trail. From about 1710, it became customary to pin the train up. The construction of the mantua was altered so that once the train was pinned up, the reverse of the train was exposed[16]. In the Victoria & Albert Museum and also other European and American collections one can find examples of such a dress from the years 1710–1720, sewn from fabric with large, fancy patterns, reminiscent of the Japanese fabic.[17]

Interiors

Activity of the Dutch East India Company (Vereenigde Oostindische Compagnie) VOC [English. nieder.] founded in 1602 reached its peak in craft imports between 1650–1730. The imported objects found their place in many European residences that began to transform under the influence of oriental aesthetics.[18] The art of the Far East since the late seventeenth century (ceramics, silks, chintz) had an impact not only on patterns but also on the material culture of that time.[19] In addition to the custom of drinking tea, enriching European cuisine with new flavours, spices and dishes, it also influenced aesthetic tastes.[20] Cotton fabrics, cheap and used mainly for underwear and linings, in its version imported the from East became a luxury product, a fashionable element of aristocratic interiors. They were used for wall coverings, valances, bedroom decorations. Their presence in the interior testified to the position and prestige of the owner.[21]

The war against the import of goods by the Indian Company began as early as the late seventeenth century. England prohibited the import of printed cotton

---

[14] Miller (2007: 161).

[15] Orsi Landini (2007: 205); Waugh (1987 s. 65–66).

[16] In the *Guardaroba Medicea* the first *mantue* appeared in 1664 and were defined as "fashionable gowns" with matching petticoats and bodice.The term "manto" appeared on 20 June 1674; Orsi Landini (2007: 205).

[17] Metropolitan Museum of Art inv. no (1991.6.1a, b); Los Angeles County Museum of Art, inv. no M.88.39a-c.

[18] Grimm (2007: 77–90); Kilarska (1981: 83–105).

[19] Miller (2007: 161).

[20] Miller (2007: 161); Bogucka (1997: 157).

[21] Grimm (2007: 77– 90).

in 1700 while France issued a ban on import of silk from China in 1702. In Prussia, Austria and Italy, printed fabrics and clothes sewn from them were destroyed.[22]

The impact of patterns of Indian prints, chintz and palampur is particularly evident in the first half of the eighteenth century – in patterns of silks and embroidery. Motifs of trees with large flowers combined with elements of the landscape and architecture became very popular.[23] The first studies on the origin of bizarre patterns on silk fabrics published in the 1950s show these relationships.[24]

The colourful story of a trip to China made by Joan Nieuhof *L'Ambasade de la Compagne orientale des Provinces Unies vers l'empereur de la Chine, ou grand cam de Tartaire faite par les Srs Pierre de Goyer, & Jacob de Keyser* in 1665 became a source of inspiration for French artists.[25] Samplers of decorative patterns created at this time became a source for the chinoiserie that started to enter fashionable interiors. Chinese characters on lacquer objects or fabrics appeared as the theme but also as an aesthetic inspiration for designs. Treasuries of Far Eastern motifs were also created in the years 1660–1690[26] and in French and German residences, cabinets were decorated with *chinoiserie*.[27]

At the beginning of the eighteenth century, the import of Chinese silks was prohibited, providing an opportunity for the Dutch to enter the market with their imitations.[28] These silks produced from 1707 until 1710 in Holland can be distinguished by two features: satin woven ground and a width of 78 cm within the selvage – wider than the silks manufactured in other European countries.[29] Besides the chinoiserie pattern, their width was to convince buyers that they had bought silk from the Far East.[30] In addition to the samples from the Richelieu collection that were first attributed to Dutch workshops, in other European collections there are also fragments of these silks which have their whole width preserved.[31] In the National Museum in Warsaw we also possess such Dutch products[32] (ill. 7) – for example, a silk with the strange fragments of architecture (masts) and the second with a theme of classic *chinoiserie*. An interesting

22 Farrell (2013: 138–140).
23 Szewczyk-Prokurat (2010: 392).
24 Slomann, (1953); Thornton (1958: 265–270).
25 Miller (2007: 157–160).
26 Grimm (2007: 77–90).
27 Grimm (2007: 77–90); Schwarz (2007: 91–104).
28 Jolly (2007: 115–126); Miller (2007: 159).
29 Colenbrander (2007: 130).
30 (2007: 130).
31 Rothstein (1964: 152–171); Jolly (2007: 125).
32 In The National Museum in Warsaw collection are two objects made of wide with Chinese pattern silk: cope inv. no. SZT 2578 and hanging inv. no. SZT 2387; Jolly (2007: 120–121).

Ill. 7. These silks produced from 1707 until 1710 in Holland had satin ground and width 78 cm within the selvage – wider than silks manufactured in other European countries. A taste for this type of design is also visible in the engraved glass and decorations of Dutch porcelain; inv. no. SZT 2578

Ill. 8. Cope. Silk with three-dimensional pattern. This compositions appear in pattern from the years 1735–1745, which was a development of the Jean Ravel`s style. Framed scene creates three-dimensional effect Chinoiserie and pseudo-oriental ornaments; inv. no. SZT 2964

collection of Dutch silks (with their signature weaving) is found in the Abegg-Stifftung (ill. 9).[33]

Chinoiserie and pseudo-oriental ornaments also appeared in so-called three-dimensional patterns. A taste for this type of design is also visible in the engraved glass and decorations of Dutch porcelain.[34] The inspiration for the decorations are the graphics of Esaias Johannes Nilson (1721–1788) depicting oriental-looking figures arranged in a roccail frame. One piece of fabric with such a design is kept in the National Museum in Warsaw collection (ill. 8). Similar compositions appeared in a pattern from the years 1735–1745, which was a development of Jean Ravel`s style with a framed scene creating a three-dimensional effect.

[33] Miller (2007: 116–126).
[34] Miller (2007: 116–126) Kilarska (1981: 83–105).

Ill. 9.
Dutch bizarre silk, piece of hanging; inv. no. SZT 2387

With oriental elements in their design, Dutch silks in the first half of the eighteenth century were so popular and interesting for the European market. The current search for mutal links and influences of European and Japanese craft can include the Japanese *Rimpa school*. This is evident not only in the design but also in the transfer of some of the techniques and their textural and visual effects.[35]

It is possible to see the inspirations drawn from the technique: Shibori, *kasuri* and Japanese gold embroidery *nuihaku* as well as the application of Surihaku.[36] This is evident not only in the first half of the eighteenth century, in the period of greatest influence, but even in the 1690s too.

The similarity to the delicate openwork-style background created by a technique called *shiborii* is visible in patterns of lace-decorated fabrics produced in the 1720. Until not only elements of French laces patterns had been seen as an inspiration

[35] Miller (2007: 156–160, 163).
[36] Miller (2007: 163).

there.[37] The influence of patterns created according to the *shibori* technique can be observed in the *drogets* produced in the sixties.[38] Ovals covered with fine patterns are linked by fine miniature stylised floral motifs that fill the entire surface. Mostly men's garments were sewn in these fabrics, filled with fine ornaments forms[39] – between the pattern of flowering branches with flowers in a geometrical form – also appearing in England silks in the forties.

In the first half of the eighteenth century floral patterns appeared, inspired by Indian prints both in terms of the embroidery patterns and techniques. Referring to the fantastic composition of palampores with the tree of life motif, they decorated secular and liturgical vestments. Some elements also show a similarity to motifs from pattern books for Kosode decoration.[40]

The influence of art of the Far East, and especially Japan, was much stronger and deeper than merely copying motifs and compositions. Japanese artists created output in any media without a preference for painting or crafts.[41] Such a way of thinking threw a different perspective on art. Each object – vase, fan, screen, furniture – could be a motif or part of a composition. Items referred to each other. Such poetics were incomprehensible to the Western mind. Transmitted by artists from object to object, the decorations were astonishing in terms of their distinctness and fantasy. They became the values that would become a permanent part of Rococo art, casing a whole new perspective on arts and crafts.

Bibliography

Ackermann 2000 = Hans Christoph Ackermann,. *Seidengewebe des 18. Jahrhunderts vol. I Bizarre Seiden.* Textilsammlung der Abegg-Stiftung Volume 2, Riggisberg: Abegg-Stiftung, 2000.

Bailey 1999 = *Kaempfer, Engelbert, Kaempfer's Japan: Tokugawa Culture Observed,* Edited, translated, and annotated by Beatrice M. Bodart- Bailey, Honolulu: University of Hawaii Press 1999.

Bogucka 1997 = Maria Bogucka, *Żyć w dawnym Gdańsku* (Live in former Gdansk), Warszawa: Wydawnictwo TRIO, 1997.

Colenbrander 2007 = Sjoukje Colenbrander and Clare Browne, "Indiennes: *Chinoiserie* Silks with Woven Inscriptions", "Exotic, Foreign Influences on Early Eighteenth-Century Silk designs", *Riggisberger Berichte,* no. 14, Riggisberg: Abegg-Stiftung, 2007.

Farrell 2013 = William Farrell, "Silk and Globalization in Eighteenth-Century London: Commodities, People and Connection sc. 1720–1800", William Farrell Thesis

---

[37] Miller (2007: 163).
[38] Orlińska-Mianowska (2003: 49).
[39] Orlińska-Mianowska (2003, p. 49, 90).
[40] Miller (2007: 162–163).
[41] Kubiak Ho-Chi (Kraków 2009: 67, 71).

submitted for the degree of PhD, Historical Research, Birkbeck, London: University of London, 2013.
http://bbktheses.da.ulcc.ac.uk/58/1/cp_Farrell_thesis_silk_2013_v.2.pdf, (entry: 23.11.15)
Fukai 1994 = Akiko Fukai, *Japonism in Fashion*, Kyoto Costume Institute
http://www.kci.or.jp/research/dresstudy/pdf/e_Fukai_Japonism_in_Fashion.pdf (entry: 23.09.16).

Grimm 2007 = Ulrike Grimm, "Favorite, a Rare Palace Exuding the Spirit of an Age When Chinoiserie Reignet Supreme", "Taste for the Exotic, Foreign Influences on Early Eighteenth-Century Silk Designs", *Riggisberger Berichte*, no. 14, Riggisberg: Abegg-Stiftung, 2007.

Hayao 1988 = Ishimura Hayao, Marauyama Nobuhiko *Robes of Elegance, Japanese Kimonos of the 16th–20th Centuries,* Raleigh: North Carolina Museum of Art, 1988.

Jolly 2007 = Anna Jolly " A Group of Chinoiserie Silk Woven in Amsterdam", Taste for the Exotic, "Foreign Influences on Early Eighteenth-Century Silk Designs" *Riggisberger Berichte,* no. 14, Riggisberg: Abegg-Stiftung, 2007.

Kilarska 1981 = Elżbieta Kilarska' "Dalekowschodnie motywy figuralne na ceramice pomorskiej w drugiej ćwierci XVIII wieku" (Far Istern Figural Motifs on Pomeranian Pottery in The first half of The 18th Century), *Gdańskie studia muzealne* (Gdansk Museum Studies), vol. 3, Gdańsk: Muzeum Narodowe w Gdańsku, 1981.

Kubiak Ho-Chi 2009 = Beata Kubiak Ho-Chi *Estetyka i sztuka japońska, wybrane zagadnienia, (Aesthetics and Japanese art, selected issues),* Kraków: Universitas, 2009.

Leclercq 2001 = Jean-Paul Leclercq, *Jouer la lumiére,* Catalogue de l'exposition présentée au Musée de la Mode et du Textile du 25 janvier 2001 au 2 janvier 2002. (Catalogue of the exhibition presented at the Fashion and Textile Museum of January 25, 2001 to January 2, 2002); Paris: Musée de la Mode et du Textile et Adam Biro, 2001.

Leclercq 2007 = Jean- Paul Leclercq, "From Threads to Pattern Composition, Technique, and Aesthetics", " A Taste for the Exotic, Foreign Influences on Early Eighteenth-Century Silk Designs", *Riggisberger Berichte,* no. 14, Riggisberg: Abegg-Stiftung, 2007, pp. 139–154.

Miller 2007 = Susan Miller, "Europa looks East; Ceramics and Silks, 1680–1710", "A Taste for the Exotic Foreign Influences on Early Eighteenth-Century Silk Designs", *Riggisberger Berichte,* no. 14, Riggisberg: Abegg-Stiftung, 2007, p. 155–174.

Mortier 1991 = Bianka M. du Mortier, "Silk Japonsche Rockts in Holland in the Seventeenth and Eighteenth Century", *Dresstudy,* no. 21 (1 April 1992).

Orlińska-Mianowska 2001 = Ewa Orlińska-Mianowska, „Tkaniny typu 'bizarre' w zbiorach MNW"(Bizarre textiles in National Museum of Warsaw Collection), *Rzemiosło artystyczne* (Arts and Crafts), Materiały Sesji Oddziału Warszawskiego Stowarzyszenia Historyków Sztuki (Materials Session of the Warsaw Branch of the Association of Art Historians), Ryszard Bobrow (ed.), vol. II, Warszawa: Stowarzyszenie Historyków Sztuki, 2001: 197–211.

Orlińska-Mianowska 2003 = Ewa Orlińska-Mianowska, *Modny Świat XVIII i początku XIX wieku, katalog ubiorów z XVIII i początku XIX wieku z kolekcji MNW (*Fashion world of the 18th and early 19th century), Warszawa: Muzeum Narodowe w Warszawie, 2003

Orsi Landini 2007 = Roberta Orsi Landini, "Exotic Influences on European Fashion, 1680–1720"; " A Taste for the Exotic, Foreign Influences on Early Eighteenth-Century Silk Designs", *Riggisberger Berichte,* no. 14, Riggisberg: Abegg-Stiftung, 2007, pp. 197–210.

Peck 2013 = Amelia Peck, Amy Elizabeth Bogansky, *Interwoven Globe: The Worldwide Textile Trade, 1500–1800,* cat. Metropolitan Museum of Art, New York, 2013, s.5, Fig. 3.

Ribeiro 2001 = Alieen Ribeiro, *Dress in Eighteenth Century Europe 1715–1789,* London 2001, pp. 26, 27, 75.

Rothstein 1984 = N. Rothstein *Silk Design*, w: *Rococo. Art and Design in Hogarth's England*, The Victoria and Albert Museum, London 1984, exhibition catalog Victoria and Albert Museum, ed. M. Snodin, E. Moncrieff, London 1984: 214–215, 223–225, no. cat. N3, N4, N11, N12.

Rothstein 1964 = Natalie Rothstein, "Dutch Silks – An Important but Forgotten Industry of the 18th century or a Hypothesis?"; Oud Holland - Quarterly for Dutch Art History, Vol. 79, Issue: 1, (1964): 152–171.

Schwarz 2007 = Elizabeth Schwarz "Tapestries in the Indian Style: Remarks on the Chinoiserie Interior of the Holländisches Palais at Dresden", "Taste for the Exotic, Foreign Influences on Early Eighteenth-Century Silk Designs", *Riggisberger Berichte*, no. 14, Riggisberg: Abegg-Stiftung, 2007: 91–104.

Slomann 1953 = Vilhelm Slomann; "Bizarre Designs in Silks", Copenhagen 1953.

Szewczyk-Prokurat 2010 = Danuta Szewczyk-Prokurat „Ornat z drzewem życia z Archikatedry Lubelskiej-przykład inspiracji orientem z polskim hafciarstwie pierwszej połowy XVIII wieku" (Chasuble with embroidery "Tree of Life" from the Cathedral of Lublin – an example of inspiration in the Orient in Polish embroidery the first half of the 18th century) in "Amicissima, Studia Magdalenae Piwocka oblata", Kraków 2010: 387–396.

Thornton 1958 = Peter Thornton, "The 'Bizarre' Silks", *The Burlington Magazine*, vol. 100, no. 665 (Aug. 1958): 265–270.

Thornton 1965 = Peter Thornton, *Baroque and Rococo Silks*, London: Faber, 1965;

Waugh 1987 = Norah Waugh, *The Cut of Men's Clothes, 1600–1930,* London: Theatre Arts Books, 1987.

PART TWO: CENTRAL ASIA

Marta Żuchowska
University of Warsaw

Transferring patterns along the Silk Road. Vine and grape motifs on Chinese silks in the 1st millennium AD[1]

Introduction

Vine and grapes motifs are among the most popular patterns in the Greco-Roman world. They spread East with Greek and Macedonian colonisation and started to appear relatively early in the repertoire of decorative patterns in Hellenised Central Asia. On the contrary, similar representations are uncommon in Chinese art before the 6th century AD. Rare, but distinctive examples of vine pattern on Chinese textiles dating back to the Eastern Han dynasty (25–220 AD) raise questions about the origin, chronology and development of the adaptation of this exotic motif in Chinese culture, especially in weaving art.

According to the historic sources *vitis vinifera* was introduced to China during the reign of emperor Wu of Han (*Han Wu Di* 漢武帝 141–87 BC), when his envoy Zhang Qian visited Ferghana (*Dayuan* 大宛). The famous historian Sima Qian (司馬遷) in his *Records of Grand Historian* (*Shiji* 史) relates: "the regions around Dayuan make wine out of grapes, the wealthier inhabitants keeping as much as 10 000 or more piculs stored away. It can be kept for as long as twenty or thirty years without spoiling. The people love their wine and the horses love their alfalfa. The Han envoys brought back grape and alfalfa seeds to China and the emperor for the first time tried growing these plants in areas of rich soil. Later, when the

[1] This research was financed from the funds of National Science Centre, Poland, granted by decision no. DEC-2012/07/E/HS3/01028.

Han acquired large numbers of the 'heavenly horses' and the envoys from foreign states began to arrive with their retinues, the lands on all sides of the emperor's summer palaces and pleasure towers were planted with grapes and alfalfa for as far as the eye could see."[2]

Even if we accept such an early date of vine introduction to China it probably did not spread through the country and its cultivation could hardly have been successful in the harsh climate around Chang'an [長安] – presently Xi'an [西安] – in the Shaanxi province, were vine growing only developed during the last few years.[3] Neither is there any evidence that the introduction of the vine seeds and its supposed cultivation around the palace had any influence on decorative patterns in diverse types of art and handicraft produced during the Western Han dynasty reign (206 BC–9 AD). The earliest examples of using vine pattern in China are textiles dated roughly to the Eastern Han (25–220 AD) and Jin (265–420 AD) dynasty reign.

On the contrary, the vine seems to have been a popular plant in the Tarim basin – presently the Xinjiang Uyghur Autonomous Region – where it was introduced relatively early. The remains of *vitis vinifera* wood were attested in one of the tombs at the Yanghai (洋海) necropolis, Tuyoq (吐峪沟) township, dated to the 4th–3rd c. BC.[4] During the first centuries AD, the vine production in certain oases around Taklamakan desert must have been well known also in China. An account on the looting of Kucha (Qiuci 龜茲) by the Chinese soldiers after Northern Qi general Lü Guang (呂光) defeated the city[5] in 384 AD, originally included into *Shiliuguo Chunqiu* (十六國春秋) and cited by Li Fang in *Taiping Yulan* (太平御覽), contains such a description: "the non-Chinese of the city lived luxurious and rich lives. Their homes had stores of grape wine verging on a thousand piculs that did not spoil even after ten years. The soldiers drowned themselves in the wine of the successive households that stored it."[6]

---

2 Records of Grand Historian 123, Account on Ferghana (Shi Ji 史記 123: Da Yuan Lie Zhuan 大宛列傳:), transl. B. Watson (1961: 244–5).

3 According to the FAO report in 1998 important vine cultivations were located only in Xinjiang Uyghur Autonomous Region, Hebei, Shandong, Liaoning and Henan provinces (http://www.fao.org/docrep/003/x6897e/x6897e05.htm). China Statistical Yearbook for 2014 reports the high development of grape production in China since then and currently the Shaanxi province produces 607000 tons of grapes which puts it in seventh place in the whole country. (China Statistical Yearbook 2014. 12–10 *Output of Major Farm Products* http://www.stats.gov.cn/tjsj/ndsj/2014/indexeh.htm).

4 Jiang et alii (2009: 1458–65).

5 Lü Guang (呂光) was a general under Former Qin dynasty (351–394 AD) but then founded his own state, Liang (or Later Liang – 386–403 AD) and became emperor Yiwu of Liang 涼懿武.

6 *Shiliuguo Chunqiu (Annales of Sixteen Kingdoms)* cited by Li Fang in *Taiping Yulan (Imperial Reading of the Taiping Era),* translated by V. Hansen (2012: 68).

Ill. 1.
Qi silk found in Niya, reconstruction of pattern (Wu 1962: fig. 4)

It was not before the Tang dynasty, however, that grape-wine become popular among the elites and was imported from Western Regions (*Xiyu* 西域) – presently Xinjiang Autonomous Region area (新疆維吾爾自治區) – in large quantities. A new attempt at local grape cultivation was also undertaken in order to produce wine locally.[7]

Vine motif on Chinese textiles. Archaeological and literary sources

Very few archaeological textiles of Chinese origin decorated with vine and grape motifs have been found to date. The scarcity of such objects makes the known examples even more important for understanding the origin of the adaptation of Western motifs in Chinese art

The two earliest examples are silks with representation of animals and human figures collecting grapes from the vine. The first one was excavated from the Niya (尼雅) site, Minfeng (民豐) county, Xinjiang. (ill. 1) It was a monochrome fabric called *qi* (綺) – a warp faced tabby with 1:3 floats, made of undyed silk, decorated with vine scrolls, human figures collecting grapes and difficult to recognise beasts – probably deers and winged does. It is dated to the period of the Han and Jin dynasties reign.[8] The second textile was found in the tower-tomb no. 65 at Palmyra. (ill. 2) It was a polychrome *jin* (錦) fabric – a warp faced compound tabby, with rust-red and golden-yellow pattern representing vine-scrolls, tigers, camels and human figures collecting grapes, on a deep blue background. This piece of silk should be dated not later than the middle of the 3rd century AD.[9]

---

7 Millward (2013: 54–55).

8 Wu (1962: 67–68). Niya was abandoned at the beginning of the 5th c. AD so the silk should be probably not later than the second half of the 4th c. AD.

9 Schmidt Colinet et alii (2000: 145–146, cat. 240).

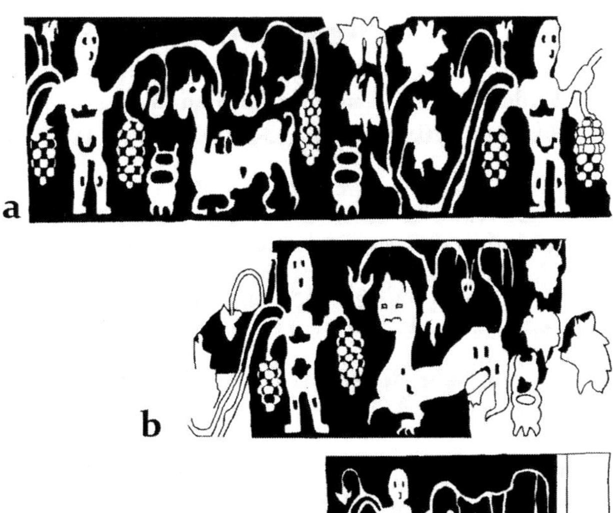

Ill. 2.
Jin silk found in tomb no. 65 Palmyra, reconstruction of the pattern on the three extant fragments (Schmidt-Colinet et al., 2000: fig. 105)

The decoration of both these fabrics is definitely untypical for Chinese textiles in respect not only to the motif, but also the stylistic features. The human figures are rough, but it is possible to recognise that on the silk from Palmyra they are represented naked, with visibly marked musculature of the abdomen – a feature uncommon in Chinese art. Such representations probably relate to images that were popular in Graeco-Roman art. The repertoire of animals is also far from typical in China – camels, represented on silk from Palmyra, generally do not appear on textiles before the 6th c. AD.[10]

Besides those two pieces of fabric no other use of the grapevine motif on Chinese silk is known from the Han (206 BC–220 AD) and Jin (265–420 AD) dynasties. Some literary sources suggest, however, that *putao wen* (葡萄文) – the grape motif – was already in use in Chinese weaving during the Western Han dynasty (206 BC–9 AD).

Diverse notes on the Western Capital (*Xijing Zaji* 西京雜記) – a collection of anecdotes about the Former Han period – states: "Huo Guang's[11] wife offered

[10] For full discussion on the silk from Palmyra see Żuchowska 2015.

[11] Huo Guan (霍光) was the high official on the Han court, during the consecutive reigns of emperor Wu [武帝 141–87 BC], Zhao (昭帝 87–74 BC) and Xuan (宣帝 74–49). His wife Huo Xian (霍顯) was involved into the plot aiming in making her daughter empress.

to Chunyu Yan[12] twenty four bolts of jin [silk] with grape [patterns] and twenty five bolts of ling [fabric decorated with] scattered flowers."[13]

Ill. 3. Pattern of *ling* silk found in Dulan (Zhao 2002, cat. 42.2, p. 107)

A little later the text mentions the production of polychrome textiles decorated with a vine pattern in the 4th c. AD. In *Records from the region of Ye* (*Ye zhong ji* 鄴中記), a short history of the reign of the emperor Shi Hu of the Later Zhao dynasty (319–351 AD) written by Lu Hui (陸翽) we can read that *putao jin* (葡萄錦) – polychrome silk with a grape motif – was produced in the emperor's weaving workshop.[14]

The question of reliability of those sources, of which first was probably written a few hundred years after the described events[15], while the second survived only in fragments included in the Ming dynasty (1368–1644 AD) encyclopaedia *Yongle Dadian* (永樂大典), and was then recompiled in the Qing dynasty (1644–1912 AD) anthology *Siku Quanshu* (四庫全書), goes far beyond the scope of this paper. The lack of evidence for grape-patterned textiles in archaeological evidence as well as in iconography before the Tang dynasty (618–907 AD) suggests, however, that such fabrics were described in the written accounts because of their rarity and unique character rather than because of the popularity of their decoration. In both cited texts such production is mentioned in the context of the imperial courts.

More abundant examples of silks decorated with the grape pattern come from the Tang period. A rich assemblage of textiles found at the Dulan (都蘭) necropolis, in the Chaidamu Basin (柴達木盆地) area, Qinghai (青海) province, brought to light two fabrics with such a decoration. The first was a *ling* (綾) – a warp-faced twill damask with a complex pattern of vine scrolls, grapes and leaves made of yellow-brown silk (ill. 3). It constituted part of a robe, bordered with silk ikat (絣) with blue and brown ornaments. The second fabric found at Dulan was

---

12 Chunyu Yan (淳于衍) was appointed as female doctor on the imperial court and was bribed by Huo Xian to help in her plot aiming to kill the empress.

13 Xijing Zaji 1.17, translated by the author.

14 Yuan and Zhao (2009: 82).

15 Knechtges and Chang (2014: 1648–1652).

Ill. 4. Pattern of *qi* silk found in Dulan (Zhao 2002, cat. 41, p. 105)

a *qi* (綺) silk dyed in yellow and green bands with blurred borders, using the tie-dyeing method, with an ornament of symmetric bands of stylised grapes represented in 3:1 Z twill on a plain weave background (ill. 4).[16]

Another *qi* silk with similar, stylised decoration was found in Dunhuang (敦煌), Gansu (甘肅) province and now is stored in the Musée Guimet in Paris.[17] The ornament on both fabrics is strongly geometrised and very far from the original vine-scroll pattern known from Western and Central Asia. In this form, on the contrary, it was very easy to apply in momochrome *qi* weve, which usually used geometric motifs for decoration instead.

A beautiful example of a grape motif is represented on *samite* silk – a weft faced compound twill – found in Dunhuang, now also in the collection of the Musée Guimet (ill. 5).[18] On the extant piece, a light brown pattern on a dark brown background forms a large roundel composed of delicate vine scrolls with a phoenix representation in the middle. Although the origin of the silk *samites* found in Western China is still under discussion, since they started to be produced under the influence of weft-faced compound twills imported from the West, and often imitated Western patterns,[19] this piece should be interpreted more as a Chinese product, since the decoration is supplemented by a small interwoven Chinese character *ji* [吉 'lucky, auspicious']. The practice of using auspicious characters as decorative patterns was popular in Chinese weaving art since Han dynasty period, although during the Tang reign it was rare. Nevertheless, the use of an auspicious character most likely defines this fabric as Chinese. The stylistic features of decoration, as well as the technical characteristic of the weaving – weft faced compound twill – suggest that this piece of silk should be dated to the mid-Tang period (8th c. AD).[20]

16 Zhao (2002: 107).
17 Zhao (2011: 184).
18 Zhao (2005: 251).
19 See Zhao (2006: 189–210).
20 Zhao (2011: 172–173).

Ill. 5.
Pattern of *samite* silk found in Dunhuang (Zhao 2011, fig. 107.1)

Discussion

There is no doubt that we can observe two phases of the adaptation of vine and grape motifs to Chinese weaving art. The first stage probably began during the Eastern Han dynasty (25–220 AD), when contact with Central Asia became more active, and lasted up to the period of the Northern and Southern dynasties (420–589 AD). From this phase we know only two examples of fabrics decorated with grapevine, both using the pattern of grape-picking silk. It is obvious that in these cases not only the vine was adapted as a decorative pattern, but the whole scene, exotic and probably incomprehensible, was copied from the repertoire of classical motifs. It could not be taken as it was, but had to be adapted to the technical skills of the Chinese weavers and the capabilities of patterning devices in Chinese looms. Generally, during the Han and Jin periods, especially in polychrome *jin* fabrics, decorative motifs repeat every few centimetres in the warp direction, while they can be quite large in the weft direction, up to the whole width of the loom – a typical bolt of silk measured around 50 cm in those times.[21] These features forced the adaptation of the grape-picking scene to the stripe decoration organised similarly to the typical Chinese patterns of scrolls

[21] Exactly 50,81 cm, Kuhn (2012: 21).

and beasts represented on polychrome Chinese silks of this period. It can be easily seen on both early silks – the polychrome *jin* from Palmyra and monochrome *qi* form Niya, where the whole motif repeats every 45 mm in the warp direction.[22] The silk from Niya is especially interesting in this context, since the monochrome patterned silks, especially during the Han-Jin period, usually were not decorated with a stripe composition of scroll and animals motifs, but used geometric patterns often composed as diagonal grids or dispersed, strongly stylised patterns, appearing regularly on the whole surface of the fabric. This uncommon composition suggests that the pattern could have derived from the other polychrome fabric, similar to the one from Palmyra.

It is very difficult to determine where exactly the original design came from and how it was transferred to the repertoire of Chinese weaving, since the evidence of patterned objects imported to China during the first centuries AD is very limited. Glass vessels could hardly have born such complicated motifs[23]; pottery was very scarce and the only type which is attested is Mesopotamian and Iranian glazed wares.[24]

The most probable category of goods which could be a medium for transferring the grape-picking scene as a decorative motif to the Chinese weaving art were metal vessels and the textiles themselves, but here we also can only hypothesise. A group of metal vessels of Central Asian production was found in the territory of the People's Republic of China, mostly in the northern part of the country. Especially interesting in this context is a gilded bronze cup on foot, with outer walls decorated with the motif of boys and birds, represented inside the roundels formed by a grapevine scroll. The cup was found at Datong (大同), Shanxi (山西) province and is dated to the 4th c. AD (ill. 6). According to Boris Marschak, similar vessels were Central Asiatic copies of earlier Hellenistic and contemporaneous Roman models.[25] Although the earliest silver dish of western origin found in China was probably produced in the Roman empire around 2nd–3rd c. AD, it arrived in China after a few hundred years of being used and handed down to various owners along the road.[26] Most of the imported metal objects are later than the silks under discussion.

---

22 Schmidt Colinet et alii (2000: 145–146, cat. 240); Wu (1962: 67–68).

23 Actually a few examples of glass vessels with painted decoration representing very complex scenes, dated to the 1st c. AD, probably of Egyptian origin, were found in Begram, Afghanistan. They are decorated with mythological themes and every-day life scenes, although a grape-picking scene is not represented.

24 A green-glazed object of Parthian origin has been found in Liaowei (寮尾) cemetery, Hepu (浦) county, Guangxi (廣西) province (Huang et alii 2013: 87–95), while late examples of blue-glazed Iranian storage vessels were found in late-Tang and Five dynasties periods sites of ancient ports of Southern China such as Guangzhou (廣州), Fuzhou (福州) and Ningbo (寧波) (Wang 2012: 85–96).

25 Wenwu (1972: 83–84), Chu (1990: 4–5), Watt et alii (2004: 149, cat.59).

26 A gilded silver plate was found in Beitan [北灘], Jingyuan [靖遠] county, Gansu [甘肅] province. It was decorated by a central medallion with a representation of Dyonisos on the panther's

Ill. 6.
Gilded bronze cup found in Datong – the whole vessel and detail of the decoration (Chu 1990, fig. 14 and 15)

Finds of textiles of Western origin with a grapevine motif imported to China, or even closer city-states of the Tarim Basin, are scarce and also date to a period slightly later than the Chinese silks. The most impressive is a piece of fabric with a grape-picking scene found in Niya [尼雅], Minfeng [民豐] county, Xinjiang Uyghur Autonomous Region. It was a woollen double cloth made of green warp and two wefts – decorated blue and yellow with an elaborate motif of vine scrolls with grapes and leaves, human figures with curly hair, wearing small mantles or loincloths, and animals: tigers and perhaps does.[27] Although the exact date of this textile production is unknown, it must have been imported to Niya before its abandonment at the beginning of the 5th c. AD. Another woollen double-cloth fabric decorated with grape and vine motifs, dated to the 3rd c. AD, has been found in tomb no. 1, at Shanpula (山普拉), Luopu (洛浦) county, Xinjiang.[28]

Since all known imported objects decorated with grapevine are later than Chinese silks with grape-picking scenes we can only hypothesise that similar, but earlier models were copied to produce *qi* silk found at Niya and *jin* silk from Palmyra. In both cases, the technological features of the weaving do not leave any doubts about the Chinese origin of these fabrics. As mentioned above, these silks are examples of transferring a whole scene that originated in the Graeco-Roman civilisation and reproducing it on typical Chinese fabrics, although we cannot exclude that such textiles

back, twelve busts of the Olympic gods and grapevine scroll inhabited by birds and lizards. (Chu 1990: 1) The dish was in use for a very long time, and evidently changed the owners a few times, it was in possession of a Sogdian owner between 5th and 7th century and later was probably transferred to Bactria, as attested by two inscriptions, to be finally placed in the grave in China around 8th–9th c. AD. (Watt et alii 2004: 184–5, cat. 90). Therefore, it could hardly be interpreted as a model for 3rd century textile production in China.

27 Jia (1980: 79).

28 Wu (2006: 213–214).

Ill. 7. Pattern of woollen *taqueté* from the Abegg-Stifftung collection. (Drawing M. Żuchowska after Bunker 2004, fig. 1)

were produced especially as gifts for allies living west of the Chinese frontier.

In later period more and more objects decorated with grapes and vine patterns were imported to China. Among them were the aforementioned metal vessels, mostly silver and gold, which eventually started to be produced locally, during the Tang dynasty reign. We find also textiles of Central Asian production, decorated with grape motifs in the tombs at Xinjiang area. The most spectacular is a piece of woollen fabric representing birds, snakes and winged boys chasing butterflies, between vine scrolls. This textile, found in Yingpan was dated, using the C14 method, to the period 430–631 AD. It is a weft-faced compound tabby (*taqueté*) with yellow motifs on a blue background.[29] (ill. 7)

Although still rare, the vine motif also started to appear in local art. An inhabited grapevine scroll decorates Bodhisattva's halo outside cave no. 16 in Longmen (龍門), south of Luoyang (洛陽), Henan (河南) province and a window frame at cave no. 12 in Yunggang (雲崗), Datong (大同), Shanxi (山西) province. As Susan Bush observed, these 5th–6th century attempts to use the exotic pattern show traces of misunderstanding regarding its nature – in the Longmen cave the artist replaced vine leaves with acanthus, also borrowed from Western iconography, but definitely much more common in Chinese floral decoration of this period.[30]

During the Tang dynasty, the grapevine became more popular than ever, and appears in diverse contexts of Chinese art and craft. The most numerous group of objects decorated with this pattern is constituted of bronze mirrors, typically Chinese objects, whose reverses were often ornamented with vine scrolls and lions – also exotic in Chinese art.[31] Vine and grape decoration also appears on silver and

[29] Actually only a small piece, representing eagles, snakes and a fragment of the vine have been found *in situ*. (Wenwu 2002: 38) Reconstruction of the whole pattern was possible after comparing it with a big fragment of identical fabric from the Abegg-Stifutng collection (Bunker 2004, Zhou and Li 2004).

[30] Bush (1976: 78–79).

[31] Thompson (1967).

Ill. 8. Silver bowl from the Hejiacun hoard. (Huawu da Tang chun 2003, kat. 40, pp. 174–175)

gold vessels produced in China during the Tang dynasty. The decoration on these objects usually mixes motifs from the Chinese and foreign repertoire of decorative patterns, although we cannot exclude that at least part of this local production was manufactured by foreign artisans settled in China. A beautiful example of such a vessel decorated with a composition of an inhabited vine scroll on the outside walls of a central medallion representing a phoenix inside and dragon at the bottom is a silver bowl found in the hoard excavated in Hejiacun [何家村], Xi'an [西安], Shaanxi [陕西] province (ill. 8).[32]

Although at first attempts to include the grapevine in the decoration of Buddhist caves, as mentioned above, during the Tang dynasty were not very successful, skilful painters achieved better results in the Mogao (莫高) caves in Dunhuang (敦煌), Gansu (甘肃) province. We find it decorating the ceiling's central panel in cave no. 209, dated to the early Tang period.[33]

Although examples of using the vine-scroll in Chinese art during the Tang dynasty are still rare if we compare them with other decorative motifs, its occurrence

---

[32] *Hua wu da Tang chun* (2003: 172–175).

[33] Zhongguo Shiku (1987, tab. 42).

in the design of diverse types of objects and its application on diverse materials leave no doubt that it was already adapted to the Chinese pattern repertoire. We even find it in the palatial architecture of the Tang era – a vine scroll composition with a hare in the middle covered bricks used for the construction of the Tang dynasty palace in the capital city Changan [長安], modern Xi'an.

The process of adapting the grapevine pattern to Chinese art manifested in its more casual use and transformations. While in earlier periods the exotic motif of grape picking was applied in weaving, and during the Wei dynasty the somewhat unsuitable pattern of a vine scroll inhabited by naked human figures was used for the decoration of the Bodhisattva halo in Longmen, during the Tang dynasty the motif was transformed and mixed with local elements. The grape picking scene and vine scrolls inhabited by naked human figures were no longer represented; on the contrary, the grapevine was often stylised and adapted to the specific features of the material and technique used. We can also observe this process in weaving art, where in some cases it is geometrised to a form in which it is hardly recognisable, like on the *qi* silks from Dulan and Dunhuang. It is also often mixed with motifs popular in Chinese art, mythical creatures like dragons or phoenixes – a composition which we meet both on the *samite* from Dunhuang and the gilded vessel from the Hejiacun hoard.

To conclude, it seems that in the first centuries AD the grapevine pattern and grape picking scenes were used as textile decoration mostly because of their exotic character and thus copied in only slightly amended versions by adapting them to the technical capabilities and skills of the artisans. It is also possible that such textiles were produced to be offered to or traded with foreigners to satisfy their exotic tastes. The more frequent contacts with foreign craft and customs which occurred during the Northern and Southern dynasties, as a result of more open trade, the immigration of foreigners and diffusion of Buddhism, which introduced multiple Western elements to religious art too, brought about the full assimilation of the grape motif, its more common use and easier adaptations in diverse branches of craftwork.

Bibliography

Bunker (2004) = Emma C. Bunker, "Late Antique Motifs on a Textile from Xinjiang Reveal Startling Burial Beliefs". *Orientations* 35.4, pp. 30–36.

Bush (1976) = Susan Bush, "Floral motifs and vine scrolls in Chinese art of the late fifth to early six centuries AD". *Artibus Asiae* 38.1, 1976, pp. 49–83.

Chu (1990) = Chu Shibin "Gansu Jingyuan xin chu dong Luoma liujin ying pan lüe kao" (Brief study on gilded silver plate recently found at Jingyuan, Gansu). *Wenwu* (Cultural Relics) 1990.5, pp. 1–9.

Hansen (2012) = Valerie Hansen, *The Silk Road*. Oxford: Oxford University Press, 2012.

Huang et alii (2013) = Huang Shan, Xiong Zhaoming and Zhao Chunyan, "Guangxi Hepu xian Liaowei Dong Han mu chutu qinglü you taohu yanjiu" (Research on the green-glazed pottery vase found in Eastern Han tomb at Liaowei, Hepu county, Guangxi). *Kaogu* (Archaeology) 2013.8, pp. 87–95.

Hua wu da Tang chun (2003) = Shaanxi Lishi Bowuguan (Shaanxi History Museum), Beijing Daxue Kaogu Wenbo Xueyuan (School of Archaeology and Museology at Peking University), Beijing Daxue Zhendan Gudai Wenming Yanjiu Zhongxin (Aurora Centre for Study of Ancient Civilisations, Peking University) (eds), *Hua wu da Tang chun. Hejiacun guibao jingcui.* (Selected Treasures from the Hejiacun Hoard). Beijing: Wen wu chu ban she, 2003.

Jia (1980) = Jia Yingyi "Lüe tan Niya yizhi chutude mao zhi pin" (Brief discussion on the wool textiles unearthed from Niya site), *Wenwu* (Cultural Relics), 1980.3, pp. 78–82.

Jiang et alii (2009) = Jiang Hong'en, Zhang Yongbing, Li Xiao, Yao Yifeng, Ferguson D.K., Lü Enguo, Li Chengsen "Evidence for early viticulture in China: proof of a grapevine (Vitis vinifera L., Vitaceae) in the Yanghai Tombs, Xinjiang". *Journal of Archaeological Science* 36, pp. 1458–1465.

Knechtges and Chang (2014) = David R. Knechtges and Taiping Chang (eds), *Ancient and Early Medieval Chinese Literature: a reference guide,* vol. 3&4, Handbuch der Orientalistik, vol. 25/3–4, Leiden 2014.

Kuhn (2012) = Dieter Kuhn "Reading the Magnificence of Ancient and Medieval Chinese Silks", in Dieter Kuhn, Zhao Feng (eds) *Chinese Silks,* New Haven & London: Yale University Press, Beijing: Foreign Languages Press, 2012, pp. 1–63.

Marschak (2004) = Boris I. Marshak "Central Asian Metalwork in China" in James C. Y. Watt, An Jiayao, Angela F. Howard; Boris I. Marshak, Su Bai and Zhao Feng (eds), *China, Dawn of a Golden Age, 200–750,* New Haven, and London: Yale University Press, 2004, pp. 47–56.

Millward (2013) =James A. Millward *The Silk-Road. A very short introduction,* Oxford: Oxford University Press, 2013.

Schmidt-Colinet et alii (2000) = Andreas Schmidt-Colinet, Annemarie Stauffer and Khaled al As'ad *Die Textilien aus Palmyra,* Damaszener Forschungen 8, Mainz am Rhein 2000.

Thompson (1967) = Nancy Thompson "The evolution of the T'ang Lion and grapevine mirror." *Artibus Asiae* 29.1, 1967, pp. 25–54.

Wang (2012) = Wang Bo "Zai tan Zhongguo chutu Tang dai zhong wan qi Wu dai de Xiya Yisilan kongquelan you taoqi" (New discussion on blue-glazed Western Asian Islamic vessels from middle and late Tang and Five Dynasties periods found in China). *Kaogu (Archaeology)* 2012. 3, pp. 85–96.

Watson (1961) = Burton Watson (transl.) *Records of the Grand Historian of China*. New York: Columbia University Press, 1961.

Watt et alii (2004) = James C.Y. Watt, An Jiayao, Angela F. Howard; Boris I. Marshak, Su Bai and Zhao Feng (eds), *China, Dawn of a Golden Age, 200–750,* New Haven, and London: Yale University Press, 2004.

Wenwu (1972) = "Wuchan jieji Wenhua Da Geming qijian chutu wenwu zhanlan jian jie" (Synopsis of the exhibition of cultural relics unearthed during the time of Great Proletariat's Cultural Revolution). *Wenwu* (Cultural Relics), 1972.1, pp. 79–86.

Wenwu (2002) = Xinjiang Wenwu Kaogu Yanjiusuo (Xinjiang Institute of Archaeology and Cultural Relics) "Xinjiang Yuli xian Yingpan mudi 1995 fajue jianbao" (Short report on the 1995 excavation season in Yingpan necropolis, Yuli county, Xinjiang). *Wenwu* (Cultural Relics) 2002.6, pp. 4–45.

Wu (1962) = Wu Min "Xinjiang chutu Han – Tang si zhi pin chu tan" (Preliminary research on Han-Tang silk fabrics unearthed in Xinjiang). *Wenwu* (Cultural Relics), 1962, pp. 7–8, 64–75.

Wu (2006) = Wu Min "The Exchange of Weaving Technologies between China and Western Central Asia" in Regula Schorta (ed.) *Central Asian Textiles and their Contexts in the Early Middle Ages,* Riggisberger Berichte 9, Abbeg Stiftung 2006, pp. 211–242.

Xijing Zaji (Miscellaneous records of the Western Capital), http://ctext.org/xijing-zaji.

Yuan and Zhao (2009) = Yuan Xuanping, Zhao Feng Zhongguo sichou wenhua shi (The History of Chinese Silk Culture), Jinan 2009.

Zhao (2002) = Zhao Feng (ed.), *Fangzhipin kaogu xin faxian* (Recent Excavations of Textiles in China), Shanghai 2002.

Zhao (2005) = Zhao Feng (ed.), *Zhongguo sichou tongshi* (The General History of Chinese Silk), Suzhou 2005.

Zhao (2006) = Zhao Feng "Weaving methods for Western-style samit from the Silk Road in Northwestern China" in Regula Schorta ed. *Central Asian Textiles and their Contexts in the Early Middle Ages,* Riggisberger Berichte 9, Abbeg Stiftung 2006, pp. 189–210.

Zhao (2011) = Zhao Feng (ed.), *Textiles from Dunhuang in French Collections*, Shanghai: Donghua University Press, 2011.

Zhongguo Shiku (1987) = Dunhuang Wenwu Yanjiusuo (Dunhuang Institute of Cultural Relics) *Zhongguo Shiku – Dunhuang Mogao ku* (Chinese rock caves – Dunhuang Mogao caves), 1987.

Zhou and Li (2004) = Zhou Jinling and Li Wenying "The Yingpan Cemetery on the Loulan Branch of the Silk Road", *Orientations* 35.4, pp. 41–43.

Żuchowska (2015) "<<Grape picking>> silk from Palmyra. Han dynasty Chinese textile with Hellenistic decoration motif", Światowit 12 (53), 2015, pp. 143–162.

Paweł Janik
Univerisity of Warsaw

The faces from Noin Ula's embroidery – Xiongnu or Kushans?

My article is an attempt to answer the question where the textiles from Noin Ula were embroidered, and who is portrayed on these garments and draperies? To begin with, I would like to introduce Noin Ula cemetery. The Noin Ula site (Mongolian: Ноён уулын булш – Noyon uulyn bulsh) is a Kurgan burial ground in the Tov province in Mongolia. It consists of 200 barrows, the majority of which have not been excavated. The dating of the cemetery is based on the Kurgans and their inventories that have been researched – from 1st century BC to 1st century AD.[1] The cemetery was discovered in 1912 by a mining engineer – Andrei Ballod – and later, from 1924, it was investigated by a Tibeto-Mongolian archaeological mission headed by Piotr Kozlov.[2] Unfortunately, the excavations were not methodical; therefore, a lot of information was lost. In spite of this, he properly identified the burial ground as a Xiongnu royal necropolis. Later, excavations at the Noin Ula site were continued by Natalia V. Polosmak. Xiongnu was a nomadic confederation, exiled on the Mongolian steppes from 3rd century BC to 1st century AD. This people were probably progenitors/ancestors of the European and central Asian Huns.

The cemetery from Noin Ula is a huge source of information about Xiongnu's material culture. Organic materials survived in a good state of preservation because of the specific conditions of the site. Some of the mounds were robbed in ancient times shortly after the funerals (the majority of precious things were lost, but fortunately not all of them). Later, these barrows were flooded. This flooding caused permafrost to form which had not melted before the moment of the discovery.

[1] Miniaev, Elikhina 2009: 28; Rudenko 1962: 4–5.
[2] Bukowski, Dąbrowski 1978: 333; Teploukhov 1925; Trever 1932.

Additionally, a layer of waterproof clay had helped in this process. For this reason, the organic remains from these graves did not decompose.[3]

Among the findings were a lot of fabrics. Fur textiles were discovered by Piotr Kozlov. During the next seasons of investigations more material was found. Until now, all the textiles had been identified in four barrows: nos. 6, 20, 25 and 31.[4] The textiles from Noin Ula are diverse. The most common are garments and drapery edgings. The majority are woollen (woven fabrics and some felt ones), but there are also silk specimens. Some textiles were decorated with geometric, floral and zoomorphic motifs. The most interesting are ones with anthropomorphic imagery, which are the main subject of my article. Ornaments were sewn appliqués (the most common decoration on felt draperies), woven or embroidered (as is the case for the textiles decorated with human depictions). These textiles have been investigated by some remarkable specialists, for example Siergiej Yatsenko, Natalia Polosmak, Olga Orfinskaya or Evgenii Lubo-Lesnichenko. However, almost every researcher has his own conception of the provenance these textiles. There are at least three dominant threads. Some scholars have suggested that the textiles came from Bactria or Syro-Palestine.[5] Others assert that they were woven in China[6], Parthia[7] or the Indus Valley.[8] Currently Natalia Polosmak claims there is also the possibility that these textiles were made by Xiongnu itself or by foreign craftsmen who served Xiongnu.[9]

The textiles with human depictions were embroidered. That decorations could have been added later to the textiles which may have been imported. This means that the investigation is more complicated. These textiles were found in all four barrows (nos. 6, 20, 25 and 31). Four fragments of woollen drapery were found in the barrow 31 (ill. 1). Three of them are fragments of the same textile, depicting sacrificial ceremony (ill. 1 A–B) and a battle scene (ill. 1 C). The fourth fragment is also a woollen drapery with genre scene (ill. 1 D). Two poorly preserved pieces of woollen embroidered textile was found in barrow 25. In this case only some parts of the imagery of the human heads had been preserved (ill. 2). One woollen drapery was discovered in barrow no. 6.[10] On this imagery two horsemen are depicted. 6 fragments with human imagery were found in barrow no. 20.[11]

[3] Trever 1932: 9–11.
[4] Polosmak 2012: 267; Rudenko 1962: Tab. LX–LXI; Yatsenko 2012: 39.
[5] Yatsenko 2012: 39.
[6] Lubo-Lesnichenko 1994.
[7] Rudenko 1962: 99–105.
[8] Polosmak 2010.
[9] Polosmak 2012.
[10] Yatsenko 2012: Fig. 6.1.
[11] Polosmak 2012: Fig. 1, Pls. II, III–VIII.

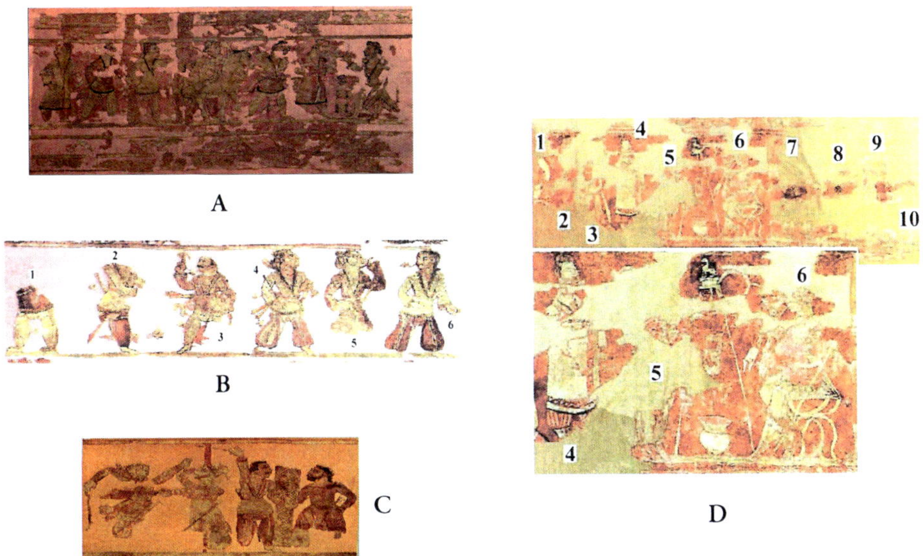

Ill. 1. A–D. Fragments of woollen draperies from barrow 31in Noin-Ula (source: Yatsenko 2012: Figs. 1–3, 5)

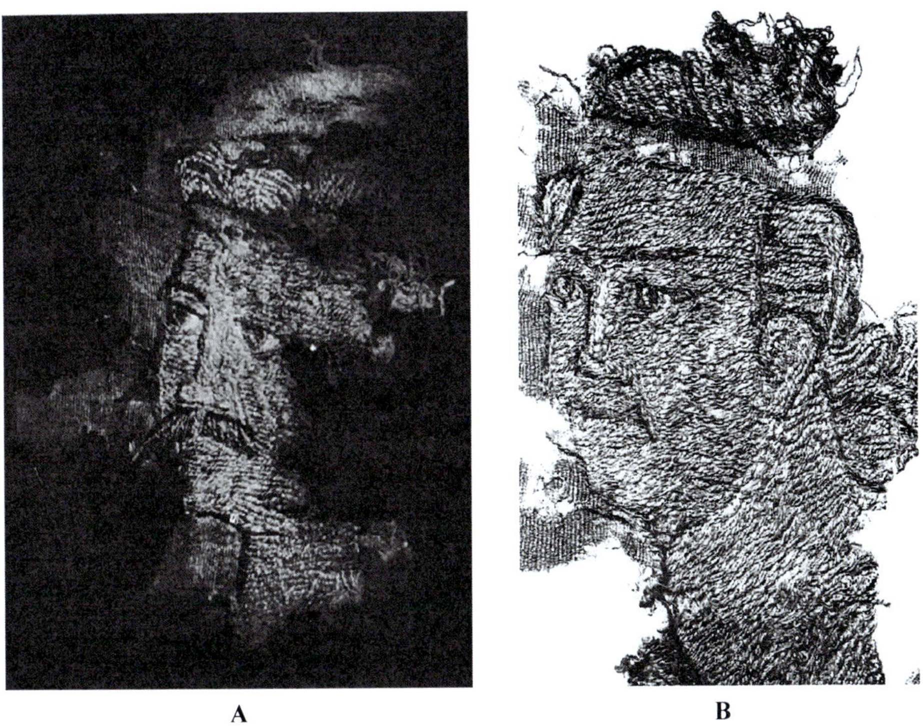

Ill. 2. A–B. Two fragments of woolen embroidered textiles from barrow number 25 in Noin-Ula with the imagery of the human heads (source: Rudenko 1962: Tab. LX–LXI)

The imagery were embroidered on woollen and silk cloths, sometimes lined with fur or leather. The techniques of all the embroideries are similar. These textiles were embroidered with couched thread. The facial features were outlined with threads of various colours.[12]

If we want to know where the embroideries were made and who is depicted on the textiles, we need to analyse every element of these anthropomorphic imagery – hairstyles, clothes and the convention of depiction. We should also consider other decorations – zoomorphic, floral and geometric ornaments.

Let us start with these two textiles fragments with the imagery of the human heads. They come from Kurgan number 25 (ill. 2 A–B). The faces are very similar, but only one of them has a moustache (ill. 2 A). Both of them wear ribbons on the heads. Sergei Yatsenko claims that these ribbons connect the imagery from Noin-ula with the Kushans (the descendants of the Yuezhi) from Bactria.[13] Certainly, ribbons decorated the heads of the Kushan rulers, as can still be seen on their coins or sculptures, for example on the one from Chalachayan.[14] This kind of ribbon is also depicted on the imagery from the Sampula grave from Xinjiang[15], sometimes connected with the Kushans. It is true that these ribbons used to be typical for Kushans. However, they were also characteristic for other nations. For example, they were worn by Parthian rulers.[16] There is some evidence that this kind of head decoration was very popular among Eurasian nomads from the Great Steppe at the turn of the millennium. It is likely that human heads from barrow no 31 were decorated with ribbons (ill. 1). Yet, it is difficult to support this notion as the imagery from Kurgan 31 is schematic and badly damaged (ill. 1 A–C). Additionally, moustaches without beards were sported by the Xiongnu too. This theory is confirmed by the depiction on the fitting from Ordos.[17]

It is not only the ribbons on the drapery from barrow 31 but also other elements that could be connected with Bactria or Iran. Some people wear long kaftans (ill. 1 A) – Some scholars claim that this kind of attire came from Iran, but another theory claims that they had been brought there with the Hephtalits.[18] This is more probable because this kind of kaftan was popular among other groups of nomads too long before Sasanian times. The long, felt kaftan was discovered,

---

12 Polosmak 2012: 285.
13 Yatsenko 2012: 45.
14 Gafurow 1978: 22, 25, 56.
15 Waugh 2008: Fig. 11.
16 Gafurow 1978: 14–15, 45.
17 Mèanchen-Helfen 1973: Fig. 75.
18 Vogelsang-Eastwood 2004: 223.

for example, in barrow number 6 in Noin-ula.[19] Another kaftan was discovered in Yingpan in Xinjiang, but it is much younger than the one from Noin-Ula.[20] Another element weighting in favour of its Bactrian provenance is the imagery of the altar of fire that is undeniably an element of Iranian origin (ill. 1 A) and was a very important symbol of Zoroastrian religion. Moreover, on this drapery there are Hellenistic ornaments and decorative motifs: floral and zoomorphic elements[21] and various imagery (ill. 1 D). We should notice that some people depicted on these textiles have elongate, deformed heads (ill. 1 A–B). A similar tradition existed in the Kushan Empire.[22] The custom of deforming a skull was also characteristic for the Huns (supposed descendants of Xiongnu). However, skull deformations were used by the Huns several centuries after the placement of these textiles in the Noin-Ula graves. They also used to practice this custom throughout other territories – in Central Asia[23] and later in Eastern Europe.[24] The Xiongnu did not practice this ritual between the 1st century BC and the 1st century AD in the territory of modern Mongolia. Another interesting element of these depictions are the hairstyles tied in buns (ill. 1. A–C, 3 A, E–G). S. Yatsenko states that hair top-knots were typical for Kushans.[25] It may well be true that they were present in Kushan culture, but I believe that more similar hairstyles come from China.[26] Moreover, Yatsenko noticed that one person standing by the altar of fire has shoes with pointed and slightly bent tips which was typical for Indo-Scythians. Furthermore, one person walking with a horse has a very long coat which was characteristic for Transoksania (ill. 1 A).[27] There is the possibility that this person was a priest. However, in my opinion this person does not have a long coat but lamellar armour, like the two people on the textile from barrow number 20 (ill. 3 A, D). Lamellar armour was typical for Chinese military iconography of the first emperor and Han dynasty times. On the embroidery from Kurgan number 6 there is also a man with a naked right arm (ill. 4). This custom was characteristic for Central Asia as a result of the high temperature but it also allowed unfettered movement (for example when firing an arrow). Yet, the ornamentation and composition of this imagery is also characteristic for the hellenistic art typical for Bactria (Yatsenko 2012: 39, 45).

---

19 Rudenko 1962: Tab. XV.
20 Bunker 2004: 30, Zhou, Li 2004: 42–43, Fig. 2.
21 Yatsenko 2012: 39–40, Fig. 5.
22 Gafurow 1978: Fig. 56.
23 Mèanchen-Helfen 1973: 360.
24 Molnár et al. 2014.
25 Yatsenko 2012: 42.
26 Portal 2007: Fig. 1–2.
27 Yatsenko 2012: 43.

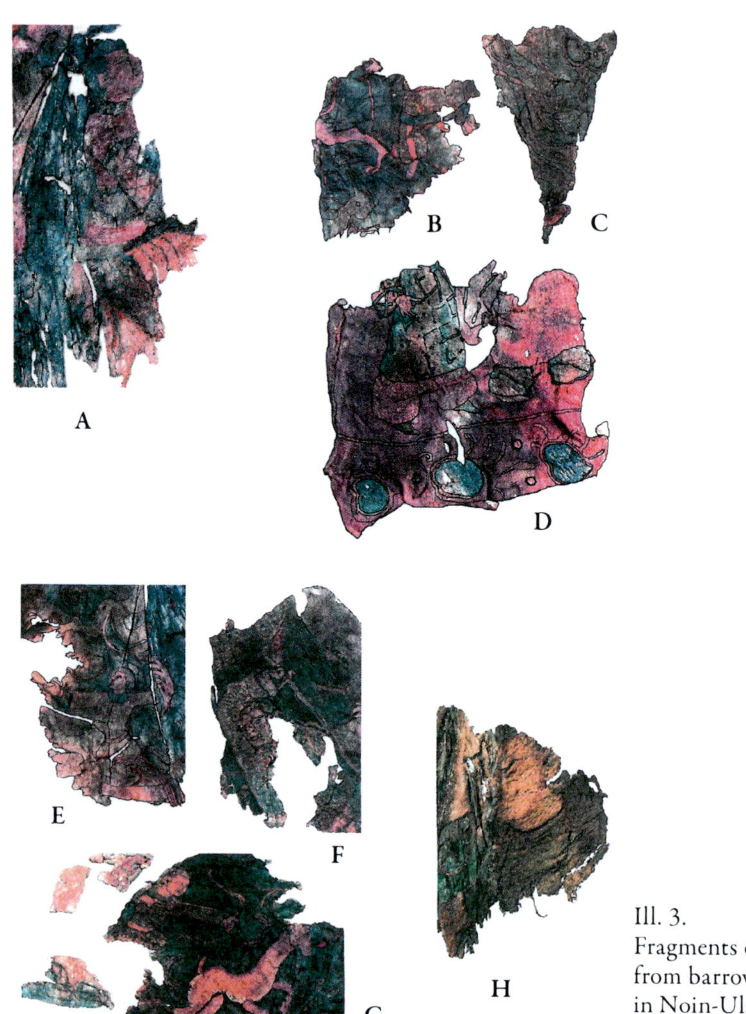

Ill. 3.
Fragments of silk fabrics from barrow number 20 in Noin-Ula (source: Polosmak 2012: Fig. 1, Pls. II, III–VIII)

Hellenistic elements also feature on another fragment of textile in Noin-Ula barrow no 31 (ill. 1 D).

Up until this moment, the majority of the textiles that I have presented suggest a Bactrian origin. However, there are some elements which are more typical for Chinese culture – for example, lamellar armour and characteristic hairstyles – and some people have mongoloid features (ill. 1 C–D, 3 A, H). The majority of the textiles with Chinese elements come from Kurgan number 20 (ill. 3), but they still have elements characteristic for others textiles from Noin-Ula (the elements that I pointed out in the previous paragraph).

On the textiles from barrow no. 20 there are several elements which came from Chinese culture such as imagery of dancing men and women, mythological animals representing cardinal directions (ill. 5) (for example the black tortoise symbolises the north and the azure dragon symbolises the east) and other mythological creatures – for instance, spirit guardians, spiritual patrons, a dragon-horse and Chinese *hua* characters.[28] In this place the *hua* character (prosperous) is combined with the *shan* character (a mountain, mountains). This may denote the character of the "hua family" or the character of the "*hua* mountain" – one of the five sacred mountains of Daoism. Natalia Polosmak tries to link these spirit guardians and spirit patrons (ill. 3 B–C), with heroes from Chinese mythology and compare this imagery to those from from the Lady dai sarcophagus.[29] On the textile fragment with animals symbolising cardinal directions/points and *hua* characters there is also imagery of four parallel lines (ill. 5). Probably these symbols represent one of the eight forms of the state of Yin and Yang.[30] These forms normally consist of three lines but the *Book of the Great Secret* allows the use of four lines.[31] Moreover, on the textiles from Kurgan 20, there is also a motif from Iranian world too – for example, a hunting scene (ill. 3 G). Such images were very popular in Iranian art.[32]

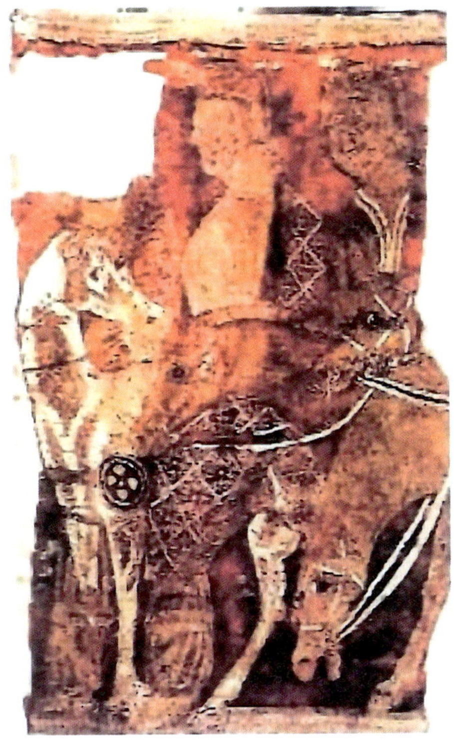

Ill. 4. The embroidery from Kurgan number 6 (source: Yatsenko 2012: Fig. 6.1)

Natalia Polosmak considers that textiles from barrow number 20 were made by Chinese craftsmen on the order of a Xiongnu noble.[33] I agree with this interpretation. However, I think that there were not only Chinese craftsmen, but from other countries or cultures, for example: Bactria.

[28] Polosmak 2012: 267–288, Pl. II–III, VII.
[29] Polosmak 2012: Fig. 4, Pl. 3.
[30] Loewe 1988: 128.
[31] Polosmak 2012: 268, 272.
[32] Litvinskii 2002: 201.
[33] Polosmak 2012: 287.

Ill. 5.
The silk edging from barrow number 20 in Noin-Ula (source: Polosmak 2012: Fig. 2)

To sum up, I believe that despite the different origins of these textiles (the woollen fabrics from barrow 31 have Bactrian connections whereas the silk textiles found in barrow 20 have Chinese elements) were embroidered by foreign craftsmen in Xiongnu state or commissioned by the Xiongnu. However, the people depicted on the textiles from barrows 31, 24 and 6 were very similar to Xiongnu embroidered on silk fabrics from barrow 20. Some people on these textiles have mongoloid features while others look europoid. Anthropological and genetic research indicates that the people of Xiongnu consisted of both europoids and mongoloids and their various compounds.[34] It is most likely possible to draw the conclusion that the Xiongnu were a confederation of ethnically and anthropologically diverse tribes. Moreover, much of their clothing was very similar to that of the Kushans and other nomadic people and their main neighbours – the Chinese. The only difference is that in Chinese imagery they were never depicted with moustaches or with a ribbon on their head, but their hair was always tied in a bun. However, there is also another possibility for the origin of these textiles – they may have come from the territory of modern Xinjiang (Tarim Basin). At the turn of millennium, this place was part of the Silk Road and there were many city-states and small kingdoms where elements and ideas from Western areas came together and combined, like Bactria and Persia (Persian and hellenistic elements), south (Indus Valley) and east (nomadic and chinese).[35] The best example of this mixed culture is the garment of the mummy from Yingpan.[36] Therefore, it is possible that the craftsmen who made the textiles from Noin-Ula

[34] Keyser-Tracqui et al. 2006: 272–281, Lalueza-Fox et al. 2004: 941–947, Lappalainen et al. 2008: 337–348, Miller 2011: 24, Tumen 2011: 23–50, Yu et al. 2007: 6242–6246.
[35] Millward 2007.
[36] Bunker 2004: 30–36.

came from the Tarim basin. This region in particular was temporary controlled by the Xiongnu. However, it is only one of the propositions for explaining the origin of Noin-Ula's textiles.

BIBLIOGRAPHY

Bunker 2004 = Emma Bunker, "Late antique motifs on a textile from Xinjiang reveal start-ling burial beliefs", *Orientations*, 35, 4 (2004): 30–36.

Bukowski, Dąbrowski 1978 = Zbigniew Bukowski, Krzysztof Dąbrowski, *Śladami kultur azjatyckich* (Cultures of Asia), Warszawa: Ludowa spółdzielnia wydawnicza, 1978.

Gafurow 1978 = Bobodzan Gafurow, *Dzieje i kultura ludów Azji centralnej* (History and Culture of Central Asian Nations), transl. Stefan Michalski, Warszawa: Państwowy Instytut Wydawniczy, 1978.

Keyser-Tracqui et al. 2006 = Christine Keyser-Tracqui, Eric Crubézy, Bertrand Ludes, "Population origins in Mongolia: genetic structure analysis of ancient and modern DNA", *American Journal of Physical Anthropology*, 131, 2 (2006), pp. 272–281.

Lalueza-Fox et al. 2004 = Carles Lalueza-Fox, Maria Sampietro, Thomas Gilbert, Loredana Castrì, Fiorenzo Facchini, Davide Pettener, "Unravelling migrations in the steppe: Mitochondrial DNA sequences from ancient Central Asians", *Proceedings of the Royal Society*, 271 (2004), pp. 941–947.

Lappalainen et al. 2008 = Tuuli Lappalainen, Virp Laitinen, Elina Salmela, Peter Andersen, Kirsi Huoponen, Marja-Liisa Savontaus, Päivi Lahermo, "Migration Waves to the Baltic Sea Region", *Annals of Human Genetics*, 72, 3 (2008), pp. 337–348.

Litvinskii 2002 = Boris Anatolevich Litvinskii, "Бактрийцы на охоте" (Bactrians Hunting). In *Записки Восточного отделения Российского археологического общества. Новая серия*, Vadim Masson (ed.), vol. 1 (20thVI), Sankt Petersburg: Peteburgskoe Vostokovedene, 2002, pp. 181–213.

Loewe 1988 = Michael Loewe, *Everyday Life in Early Imperial China During the Han Period*, New York: Dorset Press, 1988.

Lubo-Lesnichenko 1994 = Evgenii Lubo-Lesnichenko, *Китай на Шелкова Пути. Шелк и vneshnie Связи Древнего и srdnevekovogo Китая* (China on the Silk Road. Silk and External Contacts of Ancient and Medieval China), Moskwa: Vostochnaia literatura, 1994.

Mèanchen-Helfen 1973 = Otto Mèanchen-Helfen, *The World of the Huns: Studies in Their History and Culture*, Los Angeles: University of California Press, 1973.

Miller 2011 = Bryan Miller, "State of Research and Future Directions of Xiongnu Studies". In *Xiongnu Archaeology. Multidisciplinary Perspectives of the First Steppe Empire in Inner Asia*, Jan Bemmann (ed.), vol. 5, Bonn: Bonn University Press, 2011: 19–35.

Millward 2007 = James Millward, *Eurasian Crossroads. A History of Xinjiang*, New York: Columbia University Press, 2007.

Miniaev, Elikhina 2009 = Sergei Miniaev, Julia Elikhina, "On the Chronology of the Noyon uul Barrows", *The Silk Road*, 7 (2009), pp. 21–35.

Molnár et al. 2014 = Mónika Molnár, János István, László Szűcs, László Szathmáry, "Artificially deformed crania from the Hun-Germanic Period (5th–6th century AD) in northeastern Hungary: historical and morphological analysis", *Journal of Neurosurgery*, 36, 4 (2014), E1.

Polosmak 2010 = Natalia Viktorovna Polosmak, "Мы выпили сому, мы стали Бессмертный..." (We Drank Soma, We Became Immortal...), Наука из первых рук, 33, 3 (2010), pp. 50–59.

Polosmak 2012 = Natalia Viktorovna Polosmak, "Embroideries on Garments from Kurgan 20 of the Noin-Ula Burial Ground", *Anabasis. Studia classica et orientalia*, 3 (2012), pp. 267–288.

Portal 2007 = Jane Portal, *The First Emperor: China's Terracotta Army*, Barcelona: Harvard University Press, 2007.

Rudenko 1962 = Sergei Ivanovich Rudenko, *Культура хуннов и Ноинулинские курганы* (Hun Culture and Noin Ula kurgans), Leningrad-Moskwa: Izd-vo Akademii Nauk SSSR, 1962.

Teploukhov 1925 = Sergei Aleksandrovich Teploukhov, *Раскопка кургана в горах Ноин-Ула// Краткиеотчёты экспедиций по исследованию Северной Монголии в свя-зи с Монголо-Тибетской экспедицией П.К. Козлова* (Excavations in Noin-Ula Mountains// Brief Reports on Research Expeditions in Northern Mongolia in Connection with the Mongol-Tibetan Expedition of P. K. Kozlov), Leningrad: Izd-vo Akademii Nauk SSSR, 1925.

Trever 1932 = Camilla Trever, *Excavations in Northern Mongolia (1924–1925)*, Leningrad: J. Fedorov printing house, 1932.

Tumen 2011 = Dashtseveg Tumen, "Anthropology of Archaeological Populations from Northeast Asia", *Cultural Relationship and Migration of Ancient Nomads of Eurasian Steppe*, 49, 2 (2011), pp. 23–50.

Vogelsang-Eastwood 2004 = Gillian Vogelsang-Eastwood, "Sasanian 'Riding Coats': The Iranian evidence". In *Riding Costume in Egypt: Origin and Appearance*, Gillian Vogelsang-Eastwood (ed.), Leiden: Brill, 2004, pp. 209–230.

Waugh 2008 = Daniel Waugh, "Beyond the Sensational: The Reiss-Engelhorn-Museums' "Origins of the Silk Road"", *The Silk Road*, 5, 2 (2008), pp. 1–6.

Yatsenko 2012 = Sergei Yatsenko, "Yuezhi on Bactrian Embroidery from Textiles Found at Noyon uul, Mongolia", *The Silk Road*, 10 (2012), pp. 39–48.

Yu et al. 2006 = Yu Changchun, Li Xie, Xiaolei Zhang, Hu Zhou, Hong Zhu, "Genetic analyses on the affinities between Tuoba Xianbei and Xiongnu populations", *FEBS Letters*, 580, 26 (2006), pp. 6242–6246.

Zhou, Li 2004 = Jinling Zhou, Wenying Li, "The Yingpan cemetery on the Loulan branch of the Silk Road", *Orientations*, 35, 4 (2004), pp. 41–43.

Astrid Klein
Free University of Berlin

The language of Kučean clothing: a comparative study of wall paintings and textiles

Many questions arose concerning the identity of the Indo-Iranian inhabitants of the Buddhist Kuča kingdom, who lived there around the 6th to 7th century on the Northern Silk Road, in an area that today forms part of China's North-Western *Xīnjiāng* 新疆 Uyghur Autonomous Region. In the Turfan Collection of the Museum of Asian Art Berlin there are some of the best-preserved portraits of the Kučeans, of which this study[1] examines the patterns of four people's clothing and compares them to similarly patterned textiles. Behind each portrait stands a real person, whose name is given in cartouches above it. Of the people presented here, however, only one cartouche remains. How did the donors want themselves, their servants or accompanying monks to be portrayed? Which features are emphasised, which are not? Personal physical characteristics like facial features, size, stature are standardised. Did the manifold patterns in the clothing play an important role instead? Which information can be obtained from Kučean patterned clothing of the 6th to 7th century and comparable textile patterns of the 6th to 10th century and do they point to any cultural affiliation and social differentiation?

[1] This paper was presented at the conference "Textiles of the Silk Road. Design and Decorative Techniques – From Far East to Europe" (11th–12th Sept. 2015) in Kraków. It is a preliminary study to my master thesis.

STATE OF RESEARCH

Previous studies have addressed Kučean culture especially from the religious[2] and linguistic[3] perspective, using Chinese historical records or distant archaeological finds to reconstruct their history and ethnicity.[4]

The detailed analysis of clothing and textiles of the Kučeans, their manufacturing technique and patterning is just at the initial stage. There have been recent investigations from the field of art history and textile studies that have yielded an elementary description of the appearance and clothing of the Kučeans, a cultural classification, analysis and interpretation.[5] Yet, there is no correlating study that interrelates the depiction of clothing in paintings and archaeological textiles in the case of Kuča and Turfan. Yaldiz (2006, 93, Fig. 60) compares the paintings from Qïzïl to textile representations of Indian painting and to Indian resist-dyeing techniques. She concludes that because of the huge intervals between the objects of comparison, Central Asian textile patterns and decorating ornaments have been passed on for centuries. According to Sheng (1998) and Gasparini (2014), a detailed analysis of materials and technical processes could help to better understand the complex transmission mechanisms, as they are the precondition for the production of textiles and include information about the differing cultural approaches in the creation of textiles. In this way Sheng investigates the origin and contexts of the development of weave type and pattern based on silk fabrics from Turfan from the 6th to 8th century. She concludes that in terms of technical and cultural transfer, the role of the Iranian Sogdians was of crucial importance as they were the driving force for trade along the Northern Silk Road that passes through Kuča and Turfan, whereas it was the Chinese who dominated the South. Nevertheless Chinese silks were carried on both routes and therefore also reached Turfan and Kuča, as Bhattacharya (2003) notes.

---

[2] For archaeological and religious studies see Albert Grünwedel, *Altbuddhistische Kultstätten in Chinesisch-Turkistan – Königlich Preussische Turfan Expeditionen*, D. Reimer, Berlin 1912; Angela Falco Howard, Giuseppe Vignato, *Archaeological and visual sources of meditation in the ancient monasteries of Kuča*, Leiden et al.: Brill, 2015.

[3] For linguistic studies see Ching Chao-jung 慶昭蓉, "Silk in Ancient Kucha: on the Toch. B word *kaum** found in the documents of the Tang period", in: *Tocharian and Indo-European Studies 12*, (2011): 63–82; Georges-Jean Pinault, *Chrestomathie Tokarienne: Textes et Grammaire*, Paris: Société de Linguistique de Paris, 2008.

[4] For history and ethnicity see J. P. Mallory, Victor H. Mair, *The Tarim Mummies: Ancient China and the Mystery of the earliest Peoples from the West*, London: Thames & Hudson, 2000.

[5] For recent studies on Kučean clothing and textiles see Ebert (2006: 101–116); Eiren Shea Warneck, "Representations of Tocharians in Buddhist Paintings", in: Mair, Victor H. (ed.), *Sino-Platonic Papers. The "Silk Roads" in Time and Space: Migrations, Motifs, and Materials,* (2012): 156–201; Wu (2006: 211–242); Yokohari (1992: 167–183).

Scope of Research

Kuča also had an advanced silk industry and forged its own independent traditions even before Turfan, but relevant textile remains are no longer extant there.[6] Instead, Kuča is famous for its adjacent Buddhist cave monastery Qïzïl, where paintings remain that depict the Kučeans in their clothing and accompanying patterns. Whereas the advantage of painting is the depiction of clothing in everyday or ritual context, the disadvantage in comparison to textiles consists in the lack of information about the material, weave and pattern technique of the worn clothing. Documents provide information that special silks were traded from Turfan to Kuča and, on the other hand, artisans from Turfan imitated the Kučean style.[7] The numerous textile finds from the cemeteries of Astana and Qarakhoǰa in the surroundings of Turfan could thus have a direct relationship with representations of textiles in Kučean painting. Are there examples of this close cultural relationship in the patterned clothing from the paintings from Qïzïl and the textile patterns from Turfan?

The rhombic pattern in a monk's robe and two silks

In the Devil's cave (C) two monks are depicted accompanying a male and a female donor. That the monk's robes show a pattern is remarkable by itself and an exceptional case: while one monk wears an upper garment with a striking four-part rhombic pattern, the other is clothed in an under garment with simple rhombic pattern of reddish-brown lines on a light background that is clearly more restrained (ill. 1a). This simple rhombic pattern is comparable with two fabrics, whose patterns were produced using different techniques.[8] The first one (ill. 1b) originates from 7th century Astana, and has a background in simple tabby weave with a pattern using the *bandhnī* technique, a kind of resist dyeing. For patterning, the light fabric was folded along vertical lines in the first step. Afterwards knots were sewn knots along a zigzag line and then the threads were tightened. The sewn part agglomerated and was thus reserved, so that the reddish-brown colour did not penetrate through it.[9] Although in geometric structure and overall colour scheme, the painted pattern from Qïzïl and this fabric from Astana are comparable, the colour of the textile is arranged conversely, and using this technique can most effectively be achieved

[6] See Kuhn (2012: 170–171). As far as I know the only preserved silk from Kuča is presented in: Gasparini (2014: 144, fig. 4): Miniature dress in gaze and samite, 15 × 11 cm, 7th–9th century, Qïzïl, Kuča region, Xinjiang Uyghur A.R., P.R. China.

[7] See Kuhn (2012: 170–171, 177).

[8] See Kuhn (2012: 240, fig. 5.42); Otavský (2011: 90, cat. no. 25).

[9] See Seiler-Baldinger (1991: 154–155).

in this way as here the line forms the pattern, not the rhombic body. There is yet another comparable fabric (ill. 1c) that, concerning the colouring, better matches the monk's robe. The provenance of this short jacket in *líng* 绫 damask is uncertain, but it was dated to the Liao Dynasty (10th to 12th century) that was situated in North-Eastern China. Its background is again a tabby, but in contrast to the above technique, this pattern is produced through weaving in an ⅓ and a ³⁄₁ twill.[10]

However, is this kind of textile what we would expect for a monk's garment? Does it conform to the ascetic ideal of the monks? Principally, the pattern in a monk's robe is an exception in Qïzïl. Usually monks wore unpatterned clothes or patched robes.[11] There is yet another representation of a monk in Qïzïl, whose robe is described as check damask and compared to a kaftan excavated at the southern rim of the Tarim Basin, in *Níyǎ* 尼雅 (4th to 3rd century BC).[12] Between the 4th to 6th century there were strict class regulations on the wearing of *líng* 绫 damasks and polychrome *jǐn* 锦 fabric that was the most exquisite material at that time. Still, there were monks of high status, who would wear clothes made from *líng* 绫 damask.[13] Those fabrics were possibly received as donations, as was a popular custom in early medieval China.[14] Therefore, the pattern of this monk's robe perhaps indeed hints at a *líng* 绫 damask, and hence indicates the special position of the monk.

THE DOTTED PATTERN IN A DONOR'S AND A SERVANT'S KAFTAN AND IN A BANDHNĪ-DYED SILK

The pattern of small dots is interesting, as it appears as a light-coloured outline in a donor's kaftan with a brown background (ill. 2a) as well as in the blue-ground-kaftan of a servant, who kneels in front of four sword-bearing donors (ill. 3a). A brownish silk with dots of light outline (ill. 2b) seems to be the textile equivalent of the donor's kaftan. Found in Astana and dated to the *Táng* dynasty (唐代, 618–907), its background is woven in a simple tabby while the pattern is dyed using the *bandhnī* technique.[15]

How this technique reached the Tarim Basin cannot be ascertained for sure, as it is characterised by relative simplicity and spontaneity and most likely developed

---

[10] See Otavsky (2011: 90).

[11] See Huo Xuchu 霍旭初, "Qiuci shiku bihua sengyi kao 龟兹石窟壁画僧衣考 (A study of monastic dressing in Kucha Murals)", in: *Dunhuang yanjiu* 敦煌研究 *(Dunhuang Research)* (2011).

[12] See Yaldiz (2006: 96, fig. 62); Zhao (2000: 54, fig. 19 d).

[13] See Kuhn (2012: 173–180).

[14] See Hiyama (2015: 81–82).

[15] See Kuhn (2012: 240, fig. 5.44).

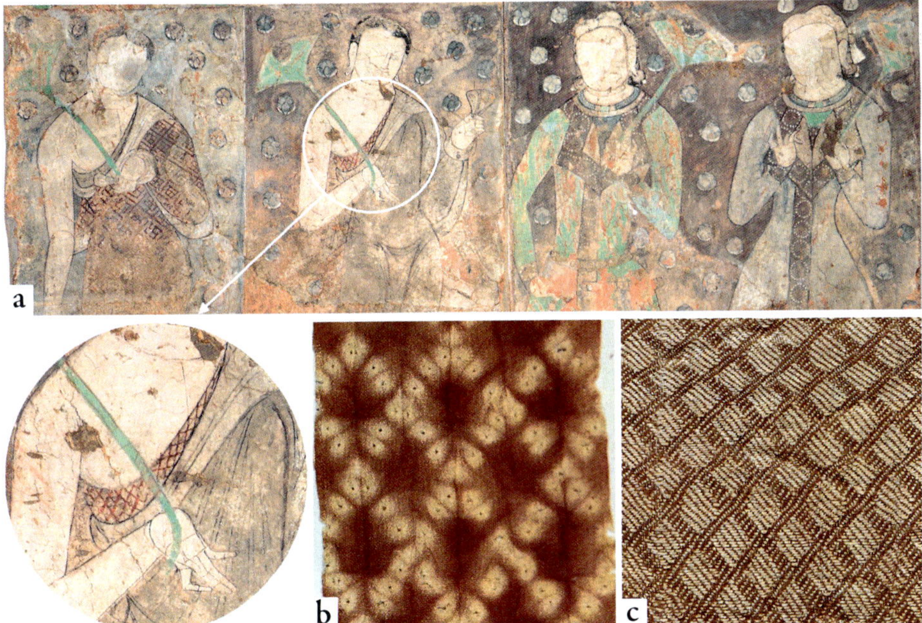

Ill. 1. Monks and donors (a) and detail of a monk's robe rhombic pattern in comparison with the same pattern in a *bandhnī*-dyed silk (b) and a silk damask (c)
1a: (inv. no. III 8428), Devil's Cave C (no. 198), Qïzïl, Kuča, Xinjiang Uyghur A.R., P.R. China, 6th–7th c., © Turfan Collection, Museum für Asiatische Kunst, Berlin (Photo: Astrid Klein)
1b: 69TAM117, Astana, Turfan, Xinjiang Uyghur A.R., P.R. China, 683 AD, © Xinjiang Uyghur A.R. Museum, Urumqi (Reproduced from: Kuhn 2012: 240, fig. 5.42)
1c: Silk damask with rhombic pattern (inv. no. 4451), Site unknown, Liao dynasty (907–1125), © Abegg-Stiftung, CH-3132 Riggisberg, 1998 (Photo: Christoph von Viràg)

in several places independently from each other.[16] For the Tarim Basin it is to believe that there was an influence from India as there was a huge demand and appreciation for Indian goods in Central Asia and in the field of textile, Indian vocabulary was used as well.[17] The Indian book *Harṣacarita* by Banabhatta, and wall paintings from the Buddhist monastery in Central Indian Ajanta document the application of the technique in the 7th century.[18] The Sogdians, who dominated the trading network at the northern rim of the Tarim Basin could have transferred the technique and

---

16 See Bhattacharya (2003: 25): For example, also in Japan, where the technique is called *shibori*, it is said to have existed since prehistoric times.

17 Bhattacharya (2003: 23–24): For example "(...) *paṭa* is a general term, denoting a wide range of silk varieties, frequently used in both Central Asia and India.

18 See Bhattacharya (2003: 25–26); Yaldiz (2006: 93, fig. 60).

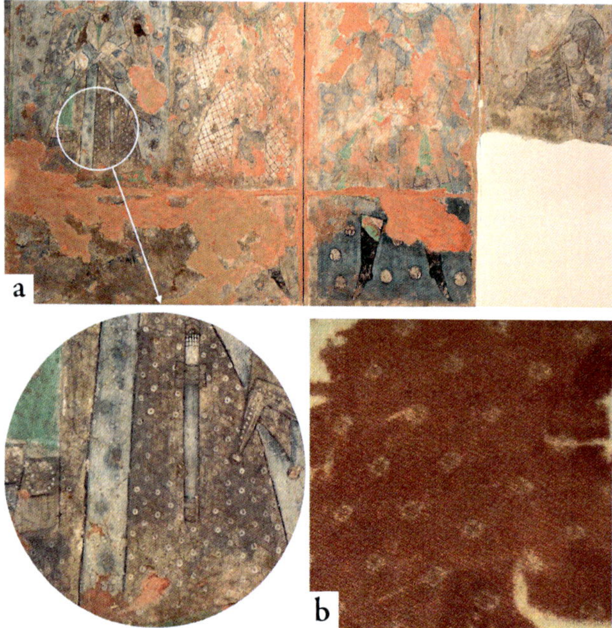

Ill. 2.
Donors and monk (a) and detail of a donor's kaftan dotted pattern in comparison with the same pattern in a *bandhnī*-dyed silk (b)
2a: Donors and monk (inv. no. III 8428 a), Devil's Cave C (no. 198), Qïzïl, Kuča, Xinjiang Uyghur A.R., P.R. China, 6th–7th c., © Turfan Collection, Museum für Asiatische Kunst, Berlin (Photo: Astrid Klein)
2b: Silk with *bandhnī*-dyed dotted pattern, Astana, Turfan, Xinjiang Uyghur A.R., P.R. China, Tang dynasty (618–907), © Xinjiang Uyghur A.R. Museum, Urumqi (Reproduced from: Kuhn 2012: 240, Ill. 5.44)

pattern. A Sogdian painting from Panjikent that depicts a textile pattern of exactly the same small dots also testifies to this.[19] The 7th century Indian *Harṣacarita* calls *bandhnī*-dyed fabrics a privilege of the nobility and their servants,[20] but on the other hand the Chinese "Veritable Record of Heaven and Earth (*Èryí shílù* 二仪实录)" states that resist-dyeing `began in the *Qín* (秦朝, 221–207 BC) and *Hàn* (汉朝, 206 BC–220 AD) dynasties, but in the *Chén* (陈朝, 557–589) and *Liáng* (梁朝, 502–557) dynasties both rich and poor all wore clothes made in that way.`"[21] How does the 6th to 7th century servant in Qïzïl fit with these contradictory statements? Does he wear the dotted kaftan as a member of the nobility or, because at that time this kind of patterned clothing had spread amongst the poor as well? The fact that in another group of people a donor wears the same pattern could be an argument for both theses. However, social differentiation seems to play a role in the case of the servant. Whereas the patterns are alike in the kaftan of the servant and the donor, the differentiation between the position of the two people consists in the kneeling posture of the servant. The clothing apparently marks him more as member of the nobles than as a subordinate. This would agree with the Indian tradition of the *Harṣacarita*.

19 See Raspopova (2006: 62, fig. 35).
20 See Bhattacharya (2003: 22–26).
21 Kuhn (2012: 181).

Ill. 3.
Donors (a) and detail of a donor's kaftan pattern of pearl medallions in comparison with the same pattern in a taqueté silk (b).
3a: Donors (inv. no. III 8426), Cave of the sixteen sword bearers (no. 8), Qïzïl, Kuča, Xinjiang Uyghur A.R., P.R. China, 6th–7th c., © Turfan Collection, Museum für Asiatische Kunst, Berlin (Photo: Astrid Klein).
3b: Taqueté silk with pattern of pearl medallions (73TAM507), Astana, Turfan, Xinjiang Uyghur A.R., P.R. China, 6th–7th c., © Xinjiang Uyghur A.R. Museum, Urumqi (Reproduced from: Wu 2006: 221, Ill. 158)

The pattern of pearl medallions with a crescent in the donor's kaftan and a taqueté silk

In the selected paintings the pattern of pearl medallions is the most common. It adorns either the hem or the overall surface of the kaftan and appears in different variants, one of which seems to be an example for an inner crescent moon (ill. 3a). In this variant the crescent has a blue colour that is framed by a black circle and white pearls on a blue background. It can be compared to a silken textile with a light background and a blue pattern that is interrupted horizontally by a stripe of red, yellow and green (ill. 3b). The fabric was found in Astana, dated to the 6th to 7th century and described as an imitation of *jǐn* 锦 silk. This kind of silk is a Chinese term for a variety of polychrome silks that are often translated as silk brocades.[22] In this case the textile received the attribute 'imitation' as it does not correspond to the original Chinese weave in warp-faced compound tabby, but is instead woven in weft-faced compound tabby – also-called taqueté – which theoretically results from rotating the first type by 90°. Although the textile consists of silk, weft and warp threads are twisted as in the production of woollens, and therefore it also follows the Persian weaving tradition in one aspect. According to Wu it was only produced in this way

[22] See Kuhn (2012: 523); Ebert (2006: 115): Silk brocade = *Nishiki* 錦 = *jǐn* 锦.

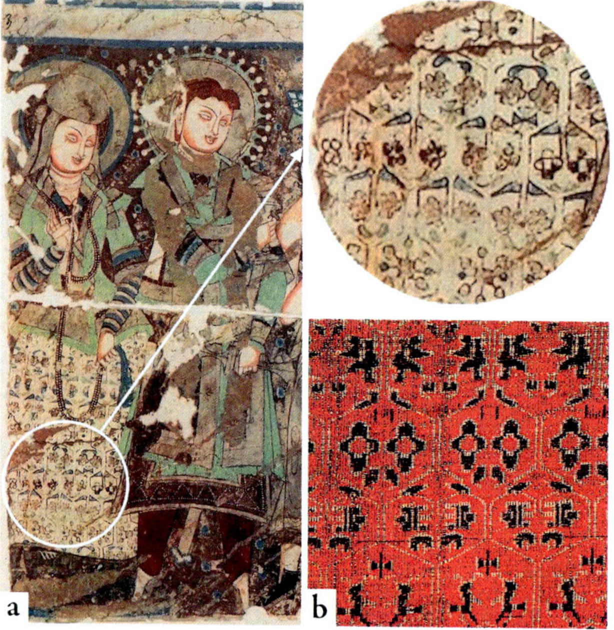

Ill. 4. Queen Svayaṃprabhā with a male donor (a) and detail of the queen's skirt hexagonal pattern with four-petalled floral inner motif in comparison with the same pattern on a silk brocade (b)
4a: Queen Svayaṃprabhā with a male donor (inv. no. 8440 a), Māyā Cave (no. 205), Qïzïl, Kuča, Xinjiang Uyghur A.R., P.R. China, 6th–7th c., © Turfan Collection, Museum für Asiatische Kunst, Berlin, War damage, (Reproduced from: Albert Grünwedel, *Alt-Kucha*, Reimer, Berlin, 1920, Plate XLVIII)
4b: Silk brocade with hexagonal pattern and four-petalled floral inner motif (inv. no. C0000494), Shujiang, Sichuan Province, P.R. China, 7th c., © Tōkyō National Museum, Tōkyō (Reproduced from: Ebert 2006: 115, Ill. 79)

in *Gāochāng* 高昌[23], that is the historical city of Turfan.[24] Documents state that during the reign of the *Qú* 麴 clan (502–540), besides those taqueté silks, some *qǐ* 绮 damasks with the same pattern of blue pearl medallions were produced in *Gāochāng* 高昌.[25]

The pattern of a plain pearl medallion with crescent is rather rare and belongs to the earliest form that is assigned to the 6th century and is attributed to Sassanian prototypes like the pattern in a woman's garment, carved in a rock relief in Iranian Tāq-i-Bustān. Similar to the case of the dotted pattern, this pattern

---

[23] *Gāochāng* 高昌 is the Chinese name for the historical area of Turfan, situated to the south of today's city. It is also transcribed as Qočo or Idykutschari.

[24] Wu (2006: 220–223).

[25] See Kuhn (2012: 177).

possibly spread with help of the Sogdians, too.[26] The particularly wide distribution of the pattern of a plain pearl medallion with or without a crescent on Kučean clothing is remarkable. The fabric of a pearl medallion with a crescent here used as a reference for comparison is, however, an exception amongst the different types with pearl medallions in the patterned fabrics from *Gāochāng* 高昌.[27] Thus, it is conceivable that this is an example for the imitation of the Kučean style by artisans from *Gāochāng* 高昌. At the same time, Kučean donors could have been clothed in Turfanese fabrics, as documents from Qarakhoja prove that *Gāochāng* 高昌 was at least one place where Kučean silks were produced: "高昌所作黃地丘慈中锦[...]。(Kuča brocaded silk with yellow ground, and of medium size, as produced in *Gāochāng* [...].)"[28]

THE HEXAGONAL PATTERN IN A NOBLE LADY'S SKIRT AND A SILK BROCADE

The pattern that shows the highest complexity among all originates from the Māyā Cave, consisting of a yellow ground and hexagons with various internal motifs in four to five colours of green, blue, orange-yellow and red (ill. 4a). It appears in the skirt of a noble lady who is characterised by her multi-layered clothing, headgear and a nimbus as a high-ranking person. The preserved cartouche above her states her identity: the Kučean Queen Svayaṃprabhā, who presumably lived at the end of the 6th century. Ebert (2006) proposed that the pattern of her skirt could be a personal ornament, reserved only for the queen. She compares the variant of the four-petalled floral inner motif to a red and black, hexagonally patterned silk brocade (*jǐn* 锦), dated to the 7th century (ill. 4b).[29] The Tokyo National Museum describes it as "*Shǔjiāng jǐn rù* 蜀江锦褥 (*Jǐn* mattress from *Shǔjiāng*)", indicating that the fabric's area of production was the Central Chinese Province of *Sìchuān*, which is abbreviated by the character *Shǔ* 蜀.[30] Distinct from the textile with the pattern of pearl medallions that is described as imitation of *jǐn* 锦 silks, this silk

---

26 See Compareti (2006: 150–152); Raspopova (2006: 61–63).

27 Most fabrics from Gaochang that show pearl medallion patterns have an inner motif of a lavish floral pattern or animals in confronting or opposing orientation. See: Compareti (2006: 149–174).

28 See Yokohari (1992: 172).

29 See Ebert (2006: 106–110).

30 See Tōkyō Kokuritsu Hakubutsukan Gazō Kenzaku 東京国立博物館, 画像検索 (Tokyo National Museum Image Search: http://webarchives.tnm.jp/imgsearch/show/C0000494;-jsessionid=1D227E6D251E572520629DDCA6D2BE68 (entry: 17.11.2015). The fabric originates from the possession of the *Hōryū-ji* 法隆寺 Temple in Japan that originally derived its collection from China.

brocade represents *jǐn* 锦 in its original meaning as it is woven in a warp-faced compound tabby.[31] The difference is clearly recognisable in the detail of the weave structure in the form of the vertical orientation that results from the warps forming the pattern here, instead of the weft.

The skirt of Queen Svayaṃprabhā might indeed have been a silk brocade like the fabric of comparison. This assumption is strengthened by a historical record made by the Chinese pilgrim monk *Xuánzàng* 玄奘, who reports that clothing in 7th century Kuča consisted of brown brocade that was worn by the king and probably by the queen too: "服飾錦褐、[...]。[...] 王屈支種也。(The fashion consists of brown brocade, [...]. [...] In this way the king dresses, too.) "[32] Still, there is a difference in the colour. The above-cited document from Qarakhoǰa mentions yellow silk brocade as an import commodity for Kuča. This would be in accordance with the appearance of the queen's skirt, whereas the red colour of the compared fabric differs from that. Nevertheless it might be another variant, comparable to the variations we see in a very small votive umbrella, also from Kuča, which shows exactly the same motif but in two tone variants of white and red.[33] Besides the yellow type of silk brocade, these colours are exactly the ones produced in *Gāochāng* 高昌, possibly also with a hexagonal pattern like the one described: "Specific types of Gāochāng silk included white-ground polychrome *jǐn* fabric and purple-ground polychrome *jǐn* fabric."[34]

CONCLUSION

The four selected Kučeans, who were portrayed around the 6th to 7th century, all belong to a well-heeled class of society – the nobility or the monastery. They are shown in religious adoration and are clothed in their best attire. Whereas individual, endogenous features are of little significance, the patterns of the clothing play an important role. The fabrics chosen to compare with these patterns consist of silk that the complexity of the geometric structure: the greater the effort, the higher the social status of the wearer or the value of the fabric. A different feature to represent the rising value consists in the increasing colour range in the case of the painted pattern, although it is achieved through a costlier weave type in the case of the

---

31 Wu (2006: 216–217): Two warps are used for this structure: a warp on the surface *(biaǎojīng)* and an inner warp *(lǐjīng)*. The warp-faced compound tabby, with its warp float covering the inner warp, shows the pattern in the warp.

32 See Xuanzang 玄奘 (646), in: Inoue (2007: 34).

33 See Votive Umbrella (inv. no. III 8605), Temple at the Eastern Gorge, Ačigh Iläq, Kuča, Xinjiang A.R., P.R. China, Turfan Collection, MAK, Berlin.

34 Kuhn (2012: 171).

textile pattern. In principle, a variability between the painted and textile pattern is imaginable, resulting from the fact that particular valuable weaving techniques are not representable in paintings. Thus, in paintings the representation of value might be expressed by means of an increasing colour range, which possibly did not underlie the textile as in the example of the six-coloured, hexagonal pattern on the royal skirt and the two-toned, hexagonally patterned silk brocade.

The cultural relations that connected Kuča with other regions between the 6th to 10th century in the textile field, can be best demonstrated by the pattern of pearl medallions with a crescent and compared with similar textile patterns, as this is an especially complex and rare design. The fabric used for comparison originates from the region of Turfan, where it was presumably produced in 6th to 7th century *Gāochāng* 高昌 and finally buried in Astana. At that time Kuča and Turfan were connected by a close interrelation that is indicated by documents that report on the trade of Turfanese silks to Kuča on the one hand, and the imitation of the Kučean artistic style by artists from Turfan on the other. This practice possibly manifests itself in the painted and textile pattern of the pearl medallion. However, neither the painted nor the textile pattern developed itself from this relation alone. The development of this motif is traced back to the Sassanian art, while the transfer to Central Asia is attributed to the Sogdians. The fabric in turn unites weaving traditions from Persia and China in its technical production.

Bibliography

Bhattacharya 2003 = Chhaya Bhattacharya-Haesner, *Central Asian Temple Banners in the Turfan Collection of the Museum für Indische Kunst, Berlin: Painted Textiles From the Northern Silk Route*, Berlin: Reimer, 2003.

Compareti 2006 = "The Role of the Sogdian Colonies in the Diffusion of the Pearl Roundels Pattern", in: Matteo Compareti, Paola Raffetta, Gianroberto Scarcia (eds.), *Ērān ud Anērān. Studies Presented to Boris Il'ič Maršak on the Occasion of His 70th Birthday*, Venezia: Libreria Editrice Cafoscarina, 2006, pp. 149–174.

Ebert 2006 = Jorinde Ebert, "The Dress of Queen Svayaṃprabhā from Kuča, Sasanian and Other Influences in the Robes of Royal Donors Depicted in Wall Paintings of the Tarim Basin", in: Schorta, Regula & Bivar, Adrian David Hugh (eds.), Central Asian textiles and their contexts in the early Middle Ages, *Riggisberger Berichte: 9*, Riggisberg: Abegg-Stiftung, 2006, pp. 101–116.

Gasparini 2014 = Mariachiara Gasparini, "A Mathematic Expression of Art: Sino-Iranian and Uighur Textile Interactions and the Turfan Textile Collection in Berlin", *Transcultural Studies* (online), 2014, available: https://uni-heidelberg.academia.edu/MARIACHIARAGASPARINI (entry: 5.09.2014).

Hiyama 2015 = Satomi Hiyama 桧山智美 2015, "Reflection on the Geopolitical Context of the Silk Road in the First and Second Indo-Iranian Style Wall Paintings in Kucha", in: Wang Zan 王赞 & Xu Yongming 徐永明 (eds.) *Silk Road Meditation* (丝路思想) *– 2015*

International Conference on the Kizil Cave Paintings Collection of Research Papers, Hebei Publishing Media Group, Hebei Fine Arts Publishing House (2015), pp. 80–85.

Inoue 2007 = Inoue Masaru 井上豪, "Kijiru dai 8 kutsu kishinsha zō no fukushoku kansuru shomondai キジル第 8 窟寄進者像の服飾に関する諸問題 (On the various problems in relation with the donor's clothing in Kizil Cave No. 8)". In: 秋田公立美術工芸短期大学紀要 (*Bulletin of the Akita Municipal Junior College of Arts and Crafts*), vol. 12, (2007), pp. 33–48.

Kuhn 2012 = Dieter Kuhn, Zhao Feng 赵丰 (eds.), *Chinese Silks*, New Haven, Conn. et al., Yale Univ. Press, 2012.

Otavský 2000 = Karel Otavský, Anne E. Wardwell (eds.), Zwischen Europa und China, *Mittelalterliche Textilien: 2*, Riggisberg, Abegg-Stiftung, 2011.

Raspopova 2006 = Valentina I Raspopova, *"Textiles Represented in Sogdian Murals".* In Schorta, Regula & Bivar, Adrian David Hugh (eds.), Central Asian textiles and their contexts in the early Middle Ages, *Riggisberger Berichte: 9*, Riggisberg, Abegg-Stiftung, 2006: 61–73.

Sheng 1998 = Angela Sheng, "Innovations in Textile Techniques on China's Northwest Frontier, 500–700 AD", in: Asia Major, Third Series, vol. 11, part 2, (1998): 117–160.

Seiler-Baldinger 1991 = Annemarie Seiler-Baldinger. *Systematik der Textilen Techniken*, Basel: Wepf & Co, 1991.

Wu 2006 = Wu Min 武敏, "The Exchange of Weaving Technologies between China and Central and Western Asia from the Third to the Eighth Century Based on New Textile Finds in Xinjiang". In Schorta, Regula & Bivar, Adrian David Hugh (eds.), Central Asian textiles and their contexts in the early Middle Ages, *Riggisberger Berichte: 9*, Riggisberg: Abegg-Stiftung, 2006, pp. 211–242.

Yaldiz 2006 = Marianne Yaldiz, "Die Rezeption von Textilmotiven in der indischen Kunst und ihr Einfluß auf die Malerei Xinjiangs". In Schorta, Regula & Bivar, Adrian David Hugh (eds.), Central Asian textiles and their contexts in the early Middle Ages, *Riggisberger Berichte: 9*, Riggisberg: Abegg-Stiftung, 2006, pp. 81–99.

Yokohari 1992 = Yokohari Kazuko 横張和子, "Turfan shutsudo Bunsho ni mieru "Kyuji-Nishiki" to "Soroku-Nishiki" ni tsuite 吐魯番出土文書に見える「丘慈錦」と「疏勒錦」について (On the "Kucha Silk" and "Kashgar Silk" encountered in the Turfan Documents), 古代オリエント博物館紀要 (Bulletin of Ancient Orient Museum), vol. 13, (1992), pp. 167–183.

Zhao 2000 = Zhao Feng 赵丰, Yu Zhiyong 于志勇, Sichou zhi lu Niya yizhi chutu wenwu shamo wangzi yibao 丝绸之路尼雅遗址出土文物 沙漠王子遗宝 (Legacy of the Desert King-Textiles and Treasures Excavated at Niya on the Silk Road), 中国丝绸博物馆 (China National Silk Museum), 新疆文物考古研究所 (Xinjiang Institute of Archaeology), Hangzhou 杭州, Urumqi 乌鲁木齐, 2000.

PART THREE: FROM CENTRAL ASIA TO NEAR EAST AND EUROPE – INFLUENCES

Kosuke Goto
Eberhard Karls University, Tübingen

The celestial lotus: on the sources of ornamental patterns woven in silk samite

This paper will identify a type of highly-stylised plant motif mostly woven in silk samite, structurally known as weft-faced compound twill weave.[1] This motif is generally described as palmette or pinecone; however, it resembles half-opening lotus buds. Its stylisation and circulation were observed on the Silk Roads in the 6th century AD.[2] The distribution of comparable patterns illuminates a transcultural aspect peculiar to early Byzantine silk weaving; the motif was introduced to paradisiacal representations in Christian art.

The motif in question is well-preserved in a fragment of samite unearthed in Egypt; its ornament appears in white cotton on red-dyed woollen ground (Musée de Cluny, Paris) (ill. 1; the reverse is showed).[3] To the right, an oval bud stands

---

[1] In a samite weave structure (based on twill weave), the patterns on the obverse are surfaced with diagonal alignment of the twill weft (i.e. warp-faced) whereas the reverse, of the twill warp (i.e. warp-faced). The samite structure is an integrated system that is composed of one type of weft that interlaces with the two sets of differing types of warp 1) and 2): 1) is a set of "binding warp" for the basic still structure and 2) another set of "inner warp" that selects a colour to pattern on the obverse, from one or more colours (up to six colours were known) combined in a single weft. On the loom, the two types of warps are alternately threaded, and both of each independently interlace with the one same common weft. The inner-warp is devised by the loom-controlled patterning heddle system that selects one colour in the plural number of colours in the weft creating a pattern on the obverse and the sorted out mixed colour remainders on the reverse. Note: all samite was woven with the reverse upper side the weaver faces.

[2] For a different type, see Goto (2015: 67–76).

[3] Inv. no. Cl.21196; Lorquin (1992: 310–311, cat 134). Reportedly from Fustat, nearby Cairo. Technical analysis: height 177 x width 200 mm, samite, 1\2 twill, 2 lats with a third colour locally. Binding warp, wool, undyed natural white, S-spun, single, and inner warp, wool, undyed natural white, S-spun doubled, in alternation. Weft A (continuous): cotton, undyed natural white, S-spun; weft B (continuous): wool, deep red, S-spun; weft Ba (extra in section, discontinuous): wool, blue,

Ill. 1.
Samite (reverse)

upright and opens six tiny volutes. A detail parallel is found in a vault painting with the Seven Jewels of the Universal King (*cakravartin*), a Buddhist symbolic image derived from Hindu art, from the Cave with the Ring-Bearing Doves at Kizil in Xinjiang, dated by a radiocarbon analysis to 431–533 AD (Museum für Asiatische Kunst, Berlin) (ill. 2).[4] Lotus rhizomes creep and burgeon on a bluish round surface. Buds open to reveal six petals in the shape of volutes to depict a moment of blooming. In contrast, the Cluny samite singles out the upright half-opening bud in the design. To the left, sixteen-petalled rosettes in lattice represent full blooms while the intersections are faced with hexagonal seed-capsules viewed from the top. This patterning thus focuses on the blooming of a bud.

Similar stylisation of Indian lotus buds is found in cave paintings from the mid-6th to early 7th century AD at Bāmiyān. In Cave 471, two volutes in a red bud

---

S-spun; weft Bb (extra in section, discontinuous): wool, ochre, S-spun. Two combinations of discontinuous extra wefts: red/blue/white or red/ochre/white. All wefts are 0,3 mm in diameter. (Note: the reverse of weft-faced 1–2 twill misleadingly resembles a plain weave. Since the red weft-faced twill obverse had worn out owing to the fact that it had been in a dump site in the old city, museums often display showing the better preserved reverse of this particular group, as a result erroneously interpreting them as taqueté; direction of diagonal alignment of twill seen from the inverted reverse as obverse; or the right and left of design inverted.) Possibly it was produced in Sasanian Iran. For pre-Islamic samite with cotton and wool wefts of this group, see Mackie (2015: 51–52, figs. 2.10, 2.12). For the technical interpretation and description, I am indebted to Nobuko Kajitani, Conservator Emerita, The Metropolitan Museum of Art in New York. For the study opportunity, I am grateful to Isabelle Bardiès-Fronty, Conservateur en chef. Ill. 1, photographed by the author, courtesy of the museum.

[4] Inv. nos. III 9061–9066; Hallade (1968: col. pl. XIX); Ill. 2 reproduces a detail.

Ill. 2. Vault ceiling painting (detail)

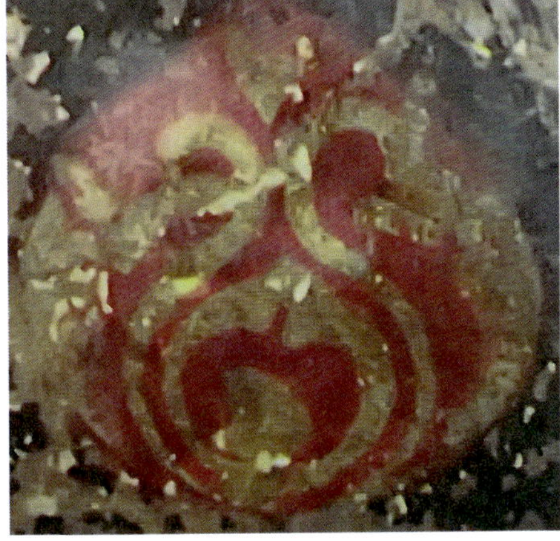

Ill. 3. Cave painting (detail)

depict unrolled petals (ill. 3).[5] This detail corresponds to comma-shaped petals in full bloom in Cave 167.[6] Variations are found in Caves 223 and 620[7] as well as in a wall painting from Kakrak nearby (Musée Guimet, Paris).[8] All of them float around the seated Bodhisatvas in blue backgrounds. This manner may belong to art of Hindu Kush which enjoyed a unique cosmopolitan style under major influences from Gandhāra and Persia.[9]

These petals are simplified counterparts to a "flamboyant" style traceable to a *caitya* stone slab carved with the Siddhartha renouncing his jewels from Nagarjunakonda in Andhra Pradesh in the 3rd to 4th century AD.[10] A flower ovary in a profile view stands upright and opens billowy petals. This exuberant image is modified to a terracotta roundel from a Buddhist stupa at Devnimori in Gujarat in the late 4th to 6th century AD.[11] It is redesigned in an upright form in a stucco pedestal from Ming-oi in the Tarim basin in the 6th to 7th century AD (British Museum, London).[12]

Both of the Indian and Hind Kush styles reached China. A ceiling relief in the Dazhusheng Cave at Mt. Bao in Anyang in 589 AD shows a large lotus in full

---

5 Higuchi (1983: col. pl. 83, 4–5); Ill. 3 reproduces a detail.
6 Higuchi (1983: col. pl. 41, 4).
7 Higuchi (1983: col. pl. 59, 2, Cave 223; col. pl. 114, 2, Cave 620).
8 Inv. no. MG 17907. Gandhara (2008: 362 in col., cat. 284).
9 For history of Hindu Kush, see Klimburg-Salter (1989: 25–42).
10 Rao (1956: pl. 52).
11 Devnimori (1960: 19–21, pl. XXII).
12 Inv. no. MAS.1098.

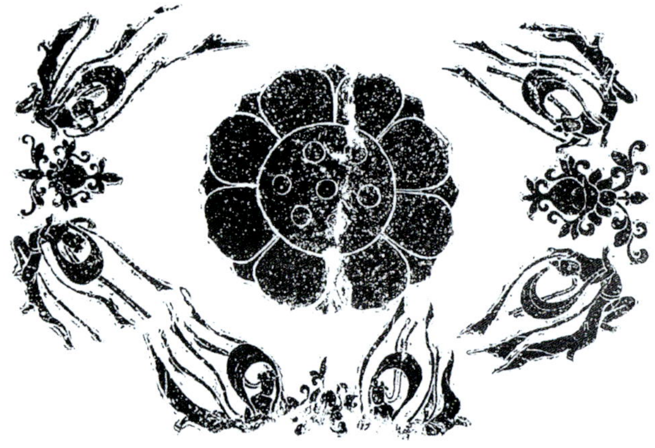

Ill. 4a.
Ceiling relief (rubbing)

Ill. 4b. Ceiling relief (rubbing, detail)

bloom emerging from the heavenly sky (ill. 4a).[13] It is encircled by three lotus-bud-composites flanked by two flying nymphs, respectively. Each consists of addorsed buds shooting in two opposite directions (ill. 4b). The upright bud has a tripartite sprout and six volutes (cf. the Cluny and Kizil buds) and contains a wish-granting jewel called *cintāmaṇi*. The small one opens six volutes widely; this form corresponds to the Cluny bud's bottom. Due to the elaborate details of the opening petals, the lotus buds lost their botanical features found in nature.

The Dazhusheng composite form is traced to terracotta tiles from the temple's paving at Harwan in Kashmir dated to the 3rd to 5th century AD (ill. 5).[14] The upright and inverted flowers are corresponding, respectively; but, the latter has a four-petalled floret instead of a bud. Kashmir was one of prominent cultural centres and neighbouring Hindu Kush; it was also a major hub to transmit Buddhism to China.

---

13 Lee (1999: 9, 12, fig. 2; reproduced in Ill. 4). For this reference I am obliged to Bernadette Bröskamp. A parallel is painted on the ceiling of the Xiangtangshan Caves, no. 7, at Handan in the Northern Qi era; Chen (1989: col.pl. 169). Similar buds are set in square lattice in the ceiling relief of the Gongxian Grottoes at Gongyi in ca. 525 AD; Chen (1989: col.pl. 72).

14 Kak (1933: pls. XX, XXX, 21, XXXII, 27); Ill. 5 reproduces a detail.

The Dazhusheng composite has a variation in a silk fabric from Antinoupolis by the Nile (ill. 6).[15] Two addorsed buds are disassembled and arranged in a roundel; four buds spread crosswise outwardly and another four slantwise inwardly.[16] Buds identical to the former are woven in a narrow band of silk samite unearthed in 'Avdat – a Byzantine town in the Negev desert, a caravan stop on the route between Syria and Egypt.[17] A jug or *pithos* with a Greek inscription was found together and datable between the 2nd half of the 6th century AD and 636 AD, the year of the town's destruction. The buds are unusually arranged in vertical and horizontal directions alternately one after another. These buds were thus contemporary with those in Buddhist art in Central Asia and China despite the long distance.

Ill. 5. Terracotta tile (detail)

Curiously, this motif is unknown in warp-faced compound weaves, the dominant weaving structures in Chinese figured-silks before the Tang era. There are stone-carved standing Bodhisatvas wearing an apron in the shape of a vertical band decorated with upright half-opening lotus buds – for example, the ones from the site of Xiude monastery at Quyang in the Northern Qi era (550–577 AD).[18] Such textile bands are not unearthed, but obviously of woven fabrics because a Bodhisatva from the Shandong province in the Sui era (581–618 AD) wears three vertical bands of the same kind terminating in three tufts, respectively.[19]

---

15 Falke (1951: 4–5, fig. 14); Ill. 6 reproduces a detail. The present location is unknown. A similar roundel is found in a silk samite (Lyon, Musée des Tissus, inv. no. 982.III.10); Martiniani-Reber (1986: 57–58, cat. 26). Its buds are similar to ones in Cave 223 at Bāmiyān; Higuchi (1983: col. pl. 59, 2).

16 This silk has also eight-lobed roundels, two different plants inhabit a lobe alternately one after another. Such a double-radiating floral composite is found in a lotus bloom carved in the Longmen Grottoes at Luoyang in 520 AD; Longmen (1961: fig. 73).

17 Baginski and Tidhar (1978: 113–115, fig. 1, pl. 21, C).

18 Yang (2004: 342–344, col. fig. 107a).

19 Diaosu (1997: 235, cat. 52, col. il).

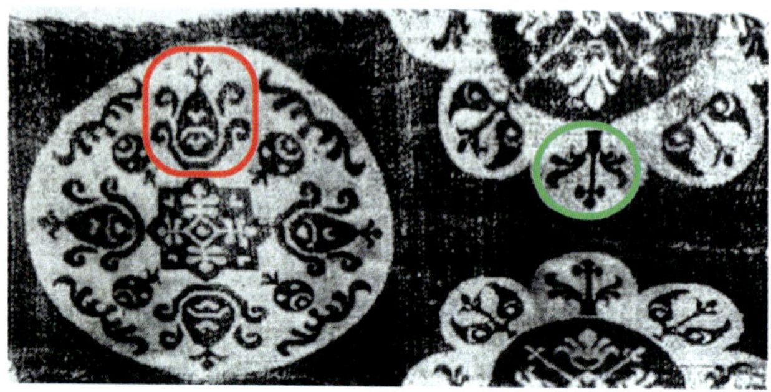

Ill. 6.
Silk fabric (detail)

Instead of such apron bands, a Bodhisatva from the Northern Qi era wears a chest pendant in the shape of an upright half-opening lotus bud containing a *cintāmaṇi* (Qingzhou Museum, Shandong).[20] The same upright buds without a *cintāmaṇi*, an intermediate form between the Indian and Hindu Kush styles, are woven in fragments of silk samite from Egypt in the 6th to 7th century AD (Museum of Fine Arts, Boston; Victoria and Albert Museum, London; The Victoria Museum, Uppsala; Dumbarton Oaks, Washington DC).[21] They are vertically aligned on a blue background and interstitial to roundels which two addorsed quadruples inhabit. Six volutes are serrated, likewise in the Cluny bud. The roundels without a border band and the interstitial buds are equal in size and this design may indicate a style before the Tang era; such patterns could be woven also in warp-faced compound weaves often decorated with narrow oblong patterns or rarely small roundels owing to technical characteristics.[22]

The question is how the Byzantines viewed the foreign lotus buds which had lost their naturalistic features. A variation of the same type decorates the vault ceilings of the Justinian's church of Hagia Sophia completed in 537 AD, on the largest scale ever seen in history. Today, the sixth-century gold glass-tesserae mosaics remain intact in vaults and intrados of transverse arches in the inner narthex and the northern and southern aisles; these three sides in the ground level enclose the nave under the dome.[23]

The vault ceiling mosaics show a medallion with the eight-armed cross at the apex which is encircled by two or four eight-pointed-star-like composites, that is,

---

[20] Inv. no. L0081. Les Buddhas (2009: 117–118, cat. 25, col. il). Wearable accessories were also associated with the stylisation of Indian lotus buds; Goto (2015: 72–74, col. figs. 19, 20, 22, 25, 28–30).

[21] Boston, inv. no. 96.347; London, inv. no. 2182–1900; Uppsala, inv. no. VM 2752.

[22] Weft-faced compound weaves can create a large pattern in polychrome easier than warp-faced compound weaves. The former were prevalent from Central Asia to Byzantium up to the early 7th century AD.

[23] There are scholars' initial remarks on textile associations; Whittemore (1933: 11), Mango (1997: XLIV).

Ill. 7.
Gold glass-tesserae mosaic

four half-opening lotus buds radiating from the cross (ill. 7).[24] This composition is found in the Antinoupolis silk roundels and parallel to the Dazhusheng cave's ceiling; here, the lotus in full bloom is replaced by the cross.

Other textile patterns are also observed. In a wooden beam of the west gallery, an original part from the Justinian era, two kinds of plants similar to the Harwan and Dazhusheng inverted flowers are carved in medallions and interstices, respectively, in a row (ill. 8).[25] This pair is found in a front relief of a limestone pedestal of a sarcophagus from the Northern dynasties in China in the 1st half of the 6th century AD (Museum Rietberg, Zurich) (ill. 9).[26] This face consists of several textile band patterns to represent a frontal. In transversal arches of the inner narthex, intrados mosaics show a series of rosette-imbedded squares and circles visually corresponding to a textile band *toga picta* worn by the consul Areobindus on his shoulders carved in an ivory diptych from Constantinople in 506 AD (Musée de Cluny, Paris).[27]

In transversal arches of middle bays of the aisles, intrados mosaics show a chain of circles and rhombuses in braids (ill. 7). Unlike common braid mosaics,

---

[24] Ill. 7, photographed by the author, courtesy of the museum.

[25] Sheppard (1965: 239, fig.4); Ill. 8 reproduces a detail.

[26] Gift of Eduard von der Heydt, RCH 115; Sirén (1959: 24–26, cat. 5). Ill. 9, photographed by the author, courtesy of the museum.

[27] Inv. no. 13135.

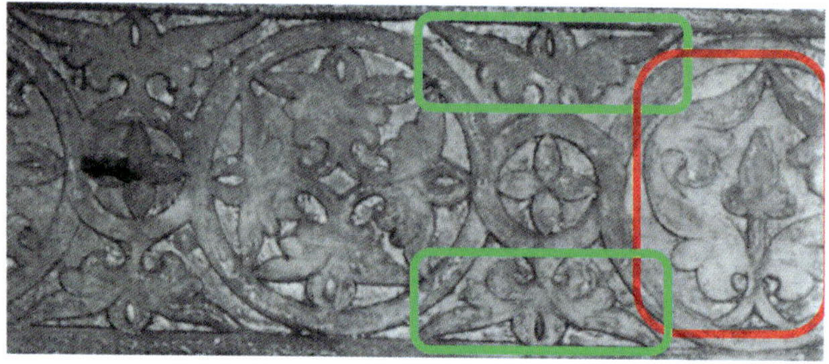

Ill. 8.
Wooden beam relief (detail)

Ill. 9.
Limestone relief (detail)

the interlaced circles are filled with four tripartite leaves.[28] A similar marriage of geometric and organic patterns is found in the narthex of the church of Hagia Eirēnē neighbouring the Hagia Sophia; the intrados is covered by a sixth-century glass-tesserae mosaic band with a series of gold rhombuses and green wreathes. A band parallel is found in contemporary stucco moulding of intrados of the eastern vestibule in the church of San Vitale in Ravenna. These patterns are traced to a textile band worn by a stone-carved banquet statue from grave no. 36 in Palmyra in Syria.[29] On the other hand, the Hagia Sophia braid bands are framed by

---

[28] Parallel band patterns are found in a wooden beam (Benaki Museum, Athens) and a limestone low-relief from Egypt (Coptic Museum, Cairo); Krumeich (2003: vol. 2, pl. 192, figs. 340 a, b).
[29] Schmidt-Colinet et al (2000: pl. 66, c).

a series of crenelated patterns. The same lines make diamond-shaped lattice filled with upright plants in a silk samite (The Cleveland Museum of Art, Cleveland; The Textile Museum, Washington, DC).[30] Thus almost all of the Hagia Sophia sixth-century mosaics are parallel to the woven-silk ornamentation.[31]

The Hagia Sophia lotus-bud is stylised with overlapped hearts. Similar four ovals extend from Greek monograms of the Byzantine emperor Heraclius (reg. 610–641 AD) and form a diamond-shaped lattice filled with upright plants woven in a silk samite from a reliquary of St. Mandelbertha in the Liège Cathedral (Musée d'Art religieux et d'Art mosan, Liège).[32] Its two-tone yellow on red suggests an imitation inferior to a Tyrian murex purple-dyed silk with golden yarns known for the highest quality of Byzantine weaving. A fragmental silk samite of a tunic from Egypt shows upright lotus-buds with six volutes and Greek monograms (Victoria and Albert Museum, London).[33] These silks recall that the Hagia Sophia foliate marble capitals are curved in openwork with Justinian's monograms and support the mosaic-covered arches and vaults.

The decorations of the upper structures are thus closely associated with clothing imagery. The vaults are exceptionally shallow and widely stretched, the same as the lost original dome was.[34] To contemporary eyes, the ceiling mosaics shone like draped canopies flowing weightlessly overhead.

It was the time the imperial court was keenly interested in silk. Justinian struggled to secure detours of silk trade to avoid high tariffs imposed by the Persians. According to Procopius of Caesarea (500–565 AD), Indian monks smuggled silkworms from Central Asia and brought to the Byzantium (*Wars 8.17.1–8*).[35] Though the details are unknown, the sericulture or industrial art of rearing silkworms was introduced around 552–554 AD and the imperial silk industry was

---

30 Cleveland, inv. no. 1951.91; Washington, DC, inv. no. 11.11.

31 The vault mosaic of the inner narthex (Bay D) has a rare depiction of buds wearing two rings (according to photographs from the Image Collections and Fieldwork Archives in Dumbarton Oaks Research Library and Collection, Washington, DC: repository nos. HS. BIA.0076, 0077). A motif parallel is arranged as an upright plant in a silk samite from the reliquary of Saint Paule in the Sens cathedral (Trésor de la cathédrale, inv. TC B 49a–c) and its archetype is traceable to Indian lotus buds in Bharhut (Madhya Pradesh); Goto (2015: 67, figs. 1, 3).

32 Inv. no. 425. Pirenne (2005: 131, col. fig. 1). Similar monograms are found in the coinage of his reign; Grierson (1968: 55, table 8, Class G; 110, table II, form k). For the study opportunity, I am grateful to Philippe George, conservateur du Trésor de la cathédrale de Liège, and Françoise Pirenne-Hulin.

33 Inv. no. 2128–1900; Granger-Taylor (1994: 122–123).

34 The dome ceiling with plain gold mosaics collapsed in 558 and it was renewed with the large cross in 564.

35 Procopius (1928: 226–231).

established by the reign of Justin II (565–578 AD). In parallel, early samite weaving spread in Central Asia, Persia and Byzantium.[36]

The lotus bud in question was exclusively selected for the vault-ceiling decorations, the second highlight of the innovative superstructure in the Hagia Sophia; the massive structural body is unnoticed inside due to an elegant style called dematerialisation. This bud motif was able to stand out because no trace of figural images is known in the sixth-century mosaics unlike other Justinian churches. It may not merely represent the lining of luxury silks but also a special meaning of its own.

Of interest in this respect is a paradisiacal image depicted in a two-full-page wide miniature in the *Codex Aureus Escurialensis* (folios 20v–21r), an illuminated manuscript of the *Gospels* in the 11th century AD (La Biblioteca del Monasterio de San Lorenzo, El Escorial).[37] This imitates a codex lining with a Byzantine purple-dyed silk with golden yarns. The design including two "Sasanian" motifs is traced to the 6th to 7th century AD: birds wearing fluttering ribbons and winged headdresses which were here modified to resemble an upright plant.[38] There are two rows of half-opening lotus buds which stand upright and contain the Greek cross in stead of a *cintāmaṇi*. This Christianisation implies such simple jewels were known as a foreign religious symbol when the prototype was designed in the Byzantium (cf. the Hagia Sophia composites).[39]

The *cintāmaṇi* was a symbol of enlightenment in early Buddhism: "He who possesses this shining jewel overcomes death and rebirth, and gains immortality and liberation. But this jewel cannot be found anywhere except in the lotus (*padma*) of ones' own heart" (cf. the Shandong pendant).[40] Lotus bud was a symbol of metamorphic rebirth. One would be born into a lotus bud and stay in the calyx of a lotus or *garbhavāsa* if one were not able to be born in a lotus bloom.[41] Stuccoes from

---

[36] For most of silk samite of this group, localisation is still difficult. The ornamentation is a secondary clue. Besides, the diffusion makes it difficult to see a subtle difference between models and local copies. Materials, techniques, and weavers moved. One should be cautious to classify Sassanian, Sogdian or Byzantine silk weaving, it may obscure diverse and intricate relations among silk farmers, spinners, dyers, weavers, designers, traders, and users. Silk samite spread probably due to the fusion of the productivity on the loom, mono- or polychrome patterning, a lustrous finish, soft and smooth to the touch, durable structure, and the reusable flexibility (see n. 1).

[37] Falke (1951: 21, fig. 136); Serrano (1994: 2, col.il).

[38] A crown parallel is found in a seventh-century ossuary in terracotta from Durmen-tepe, near Samarkand (Institute of Fine Arts, Tashkent); Pugačenkova (1985: 156–158, 171, figs. 67–68, 83, Dt).

[39] In two silks in samite with the Annunciation and the Nativity (Biblioteca Apostolica Vaticana, inv. nos. 1231, 1258), interstitial plants contain a hexagonal *cintāmaṇi* from Central Asia; Goto (2015: 74, figs. 31a–c, 32, 33).

[40] Govinda (1969: 61).

[41] Inagaki (1965: 48–51). In Sanskrit, the word *garbha* means womb, embryo, seed, and germ. The word *vāsa* means garment.

the Talim basin show lotus-bloom-born figures to represent a reborn soul in paradise (cf. Ill. 9). Thus, the lotus buds in a moment of half-opening can symbolise an ascendant pass to a celestial abode. Actually, most of the samite survived as shroud or reliquary cloth. A corpse or relic was wrapped in or metaphorically contained in a "lotus bud" for an intervening period parallel to a soul waiting for salvation.[42]

Although no textual evidence is available so far, the highly-stylised lotus bud became a symbol related to paradisiacal representations in Christian art. Lotuses bloom at dawn and close at dusk, hence they were universally related to the sun. The half-opening bud was thus able to harmonise with the rays of light, that is, Christ (*John* 1: 4–5, 9; 8:12). His association with a flower was often remarked from the late Antiquity (*Song of Songs* 2:1; for example, St. Ambrose, *Expositio Evangelii secundum Lucam*, ch. VII, 1441).

According to St. Ephraem the Syrian (ca. 306–373 AD), Paradise is a conically-shaped mountain encircled by the Great Sea or *Okeanos*. The Tree of Knowledge stands on the heights and acts as a sanctuary curtain hiding the Tree of Life located higher on the summit where the Divine Presence is settled. One can enter it if the body is in a resurrected state.[43]

The Hagia Sophia may realise this eschatological concept. The silk-drape like vault mosaics with the half-opening lotus-buds represent the veils of Tree of Knowledge (cf. the Escurialensis miniature) and enclose a luminous void in the nave; there, one gazed in awe at the dome floating high in the abundant natural lights.[44] It may reflect a St. Ephraem's verse: "Perhaps that blessed tree, the Tree of Life, is, by its

---

[42] Lotus buds comparable to the Cluny bud are interstitial to full blooms in silk samite used as the first shroud of St. Lambert, a bishop of Maastricht, martyrised in 705/706 AD (Musée d'Art religieux et d'Art mosan, Liège, inv. no. 431); Pirenne (2005: 134, col. fig. 7); Mackie (2015: col. fig. 2.24). A vertical band in samite with similar upright buds was unearthed in Moščevaja Valka in the northern Caucasus, located on a caravan route from Central Asia to Constantinople via Caspian Sea and Black Sea (The State Hermitage Museum, St Petersburg, inv. no. Kz 6770); Von China (1996: 76, cat. 86).

[43] St. Ephraem (1990: 52–55).

[44] The *Christian Topography* from the 1st half of the 6th century AD associated the tabernacle's curtain that separated the Holy from the Holy of Holies (*Exodus* 40, 1–33) with God's separation of terrestrial and celestial spaces at creation. These divided spaces symbolically correspond to the lower cosmos, that is, this world and the upper cosmos where those who are resurrected reach in the future, respectively (*Patrologia Graeca* 88, col. 56D; Prolog B'); the Tree of Life is a prefigurative symbol (*τύπος*) of the latter (col. 413AB; Logos 9, 23). See also Papastavrou (2007: 327–334). This parallelism was perhaps a source of the aniconic representation of the architectural space of the Justinian's Hagia Sophia. The tabernacle's curtain resembling the celestial sphere was depicted with holy symbols and figures in a full-page miniature of the Carolingian *Bible of San Paolo fuori le mura* (folio 32v), produced in 870–875 in Reims (Abbazia di San Paolo fuori le Mura, Rome). The domed tent of the tabernacle is found in the Byzantine illuminated manuscripts, *Homilies of James of Kokkinobaphos*: Biblioteca Apostolica Vaticana, Vat. gr. 1162, folio133v; Bibliothèque nationale de France, gr. 1208, folio 181v.

rays, the sun of Paradise" (*Hymns on Paradise* 3, 2).[45] This illusionistic space parallel to the lustrous silk imagery made the congregation experience clothing the Light or the garment of glory which human being had lost through the fall of Adam and Eve (cf. *Isaiah* 40:22, *Psalm* 104:2).[46] A cluster of luminous lotus buds was a sign of the ascension to be born in Paradise.[47]

Bibliography

Baginski and Tidhar 1978 = Alisa Baginski, Amely Tidhar, "A Dated Silk Fragment from 'Avdat (Eboda)", *Israel Exploration Journal*, 28 (1978), pp. 113–115, pl. 21.

Brock 1982 = Sebastian Brock, "Clothing metaphors as a means of theological expression in Syriac tradition." In *Typus, Symbol, Allegorie bei den östlichen Vätern und ihren Parallelen im Mittelalter*, Margot Schmidt (ed.), Regensburg: Verlag Friedrich Pustet, 1982, pp. 11–38.

Chen 1989 = *Zhongguo meishu quanji. Diaosu bian. 13, Gongxian, Tianlongshan, Xiangtangshan, Anyang, shiku diaoke* (Chinese art works. Sculptures, vol. 13. Cave carvings at Gongxian, Tianlongshan, Xiangtangshan, and Anyang), Mingda Chen (ed.), Beijing: Wenwu chubanshe, 1989.

Devnimori 1960 = The Archaeological Survey of India, "Excavation at Devnimori, District Sabarkantha," *Indian Archaeology. A Review*, 1959–60 (1960), pp. 19–21, pls. XXI–XXIV.

Diaosu 1997 = *Diaosu biecang. Zongjiao bian tezhan tulu = The Art of Contemplation. Religious Sculpture from Private Collections*, Yu-min Lee and Huixia Chen (eds.), exhibition cat., Taipei: National Palace Museum, 1997.

Falke 1951 = Otto von Falke, *Kunstgeschichte der Seidenweberei*, Tübingen: Ernst Wasmuth, 1951 (4th ed).

Gandhara 2008 = *Gandhara - Das buddhistische Erbe Pakistans. Legenden, Klöster und Paradiese*, Christian Luczanits (ed.), exhibition cat., Bonn: Kunst- und Ausstellungshalle der Bundesrepublik Deutschland, 2008.

Goto 2015 = Kosuke Goto, "The Jewelled Lotus: On the Sources of Ornamental Patterns Woven in Silk Samite," *Indo-Asiatische Zeitschrift*, 19 (2015), pp. 67–76.

Govinda 1969 = Lama Anagarika Govinda, *Foundations of Tibetan Mysticism. According to the Esoteric Teachings of the Great Mantra. Oṁ Maṇi Padme Hūṁ*, London: Rider & Company, 1969.

Granger-Taylor 1994 = Hero Granger-Taylor, "136 Silk panel from a tunic," in: *Byzantium. Treasures of Byzantine art and culture from British collections*, David Buckton (ed.), exhibition cat., London: British Museum, 1994: 122–123.

Grierson 1968 = Philip Grierson, *Catalogue of the Byzantine coins in the Dumbarton Oaks Collection and in the Whittemore Collection, vol. 2, part I: Phocas to Heraclius (602–641)*, Dumbarton Oaks Center for Byzantine Studies, Washington DC: Trustees for Harvard University, 1968.

---

[45] St. Ephraem (1990: 91).

[46] For the clothing symbolism, see Brock (1982).

[47] In the monastery of Christos ho Pantepoptēs (today Eski Imaret Camii) built in the 11th century in Constantinople, the dome ceiling is unusually crowned by a lotus in full bloom.

Hallade 1968 = Madeleine Hallade, *Gandharan Art of North India and the Greco-Buddhist Tradition in Indian, Persia, and Central Asia*, New York: Abrams, 1968.

Higuchi 1983 = Higuchi, Takayasu (ed.): *Bāmiyān. Afuganisutan ni okeru Bukkyō sekkutsu jiin no bijutsu kōkogakuteki chōsa, 1970–1978 nen* (Bāmiyān, art and archaeological researches on the Buddhist cave temples in Afghanistan 1970–1978), vol. 1, Kyoto: Dohosha, 1983.

Inagaki 1965 = Hisao Inagaki, "Padama-symbolism in Pure Land Thought: With Particular Reference to the Modes of Birth," *Indogaku Bukkogaku Kenkyu* (Indian and Buddhist Studies), 13, 1 (1965), pp. 48–51.

Kak 1933 = Ram Chandra Kak, *Ancient Monuments of Kashmir*, London: The India Society, 1933.

Klimburg-Salter 1989 = Deborah Klimburg-Salter, *The Kingdom of Bāmiyān. Buddhist art and culture of the Hindu Kush*, Naples: Istituto italiano per il medio ed estremo oriente, 1989.

Krumeich 2003 = Kirsten Krumeich, *Spätantike Bauskulptur aus Oxyrhynchos*, 2 vols., Wiesbaden: Reichert, 2003.

Lee 1999 = Yu-min Lee, "Preserving the Dharma in Word and Image: Sixth-Century Buddhist Thought, Practice, and Art at Ta-chu-sheng Grotto," *National Palace Museum Bulletin*, 34: 2 (May-June 1999), pp. 1–16, pls. 1–3.

Les Buddhas 2009 = *Les Buddhas du Shandong*, Gilles Béguin (ed.), exhibition cat., Musée Cernuschi, Paris: Musée des Arts de l'Asie de la Ville de Paris, 2009.

Longmen 1961 = *Longmen shiku* (Longmen Caves), Longmen baoguansuo (ed.), Beijing: Wenwu chubanshe, 1961.

Lorquin 1992 = Alexandra Lorquin, *Les Tissus Coptes. Au Musée National du Moyen Age – Thermes de Cluny, catalogue des étoffes égyptiennes de lin et de laine de l'Antiquité tardive aux premiers siècles de l'Islam*, Paris: Réunion des Musées Nationaux, 1992.

Mackie 2015 = Louise W. Mackie, *Symbols of Power. Luxury textiles from Islamic lands, 7th–21st century*, Cleveland, Ohio: Cleveland Museum of Art, 2015.

Mango 1997 = Cyril Mango, Ahmet Ertuğ, *Hagia Sophia. A Vision for Empires*, Istanbul: Ertuğ & Kocabiyik, 1997.

Martiniani-Reber 1986 = Marielle Martiniani-Reber, *Lyon, musée historique des tissus. Soieries sassanides, coptes et byzantines Ve–XIe siècles*, Paris: Édition de la Réunion des musées nationaux, 1986.

Papastavrou 2007 = Hélène Papastavrou, *Recherche iconographique dans l'art byzantin et occidental du XIe au XVe siècle: l'annonciation*, Venice: Istituto Ellenico di Studi Bizantini e Postbizantini di Venezia, 2007.

Pirenne 2005 = Françoise Pirenne, "Tissus précieux au Trésor de Liège," in: *Trésors des cathédrales d'Europe. Liège à Beaune*, Philippe George (ed.), exhibition cat., Musée des Beaux-Arts, Hôtel-Dieu and Collégiale Notre-Dame, Beaune, 2005: 128–175.

Procopius 1928 = Procopius, trans. by Henry Bronson Dewing, *History of the Wars, Volume V, Books 7.36–8. (Gothic War)*, Loeb Classical Library 217, London: Harvard Univeristy Press, 1928.

Pugačenkova 1985 = Pugačenkova, G.A., "Les ostothèques de Miankal', " *Mesopotamia*, 20 (1985), pp. 147–183.

Rao 1956 = P. R. Ramachandra Rao, *The Art of Nāgārjunikoṇḍa*, Madras: Rachana, 1956.

Serrano 1994 = Matilde López Serrano, *Codex Aureus Escurialensis. Documentation on the facsimile edition*, Bibliotheca Rara, Münster: Bibliotheca Rara, 1994.

Schmidt-Colinet et al 2000 = Andreas Schmidt-Colinet, Annemarie Stauffer, Ḫālid al-As'ad, *Die Textilien aus Palmyra. Neue und alte Funde*, Mainz: von Zabern, 2000.

Sheppard 1965 = Carl D. Sheppard, "A Radiocarbon Date for the Wooden Tie Beams in the West Gallery of St. Sophia, Istanbul," *Dumbarton Oaks Papers,* 19 (1965), pp. 237–240.

Sirén 1957 = Osvald Sirén, *Chinesische Skulpturen der Sammlung Eduard von der Heydt. Beschreibender Katalog*, Zurich: Museum Rietberg, 1959.

St. Ephraem 1990 = St. Ephraem the Syrian, ed. and trans. by Sebastian P. Brock, *Hymns on Paradise*, New York: St. Vladimirs Seminary Press, 1990.

Von China 1996 = *Von China nach Byzanz. Frühmittelalterliche Seiden aus der Staatlichen Ermitage Sankt Petersburg*, Anna. A. Ierusalimskaja and Birgitt Borkopp (eds.), exhibition cat., Munich: Bayerisches National Museum, 1996.

Whittemore 1933 = Thomas Whittemore, *The Mosaics of St. Sophia at Istanbul. Preliminary Report on the First Years Work, 1931–1932: The Mosaics of the Narthex*, Oxford: Oxford University Press, 1933.

Yang 2004 = Yang, Xiaoneng (ed.): *New Perspectives on China's Past. Chinese archaeology in the twentieth century*, vol. 2, New Haven: Yale University Press, 2004.

Postscript

This brief discussion is limited to explore a source of the woven patterns and would not exclude the possibility of involvement of Hellenistic ornamentation. For comparison, one may prefer stylised foliage painted in the vaults of Nero's Domus Aurea (known from engravings: Giuseppe Carletti and Ludovico Mirri, Le Antiche Camere delle Terme di Tito e loro Pitture, Rome: Salomoni, 1776, pls. 55, 57); this palace was never completed and the remains after a fire were incorporated into the substructures of the Baths of Trajan. An archetype of their patterns is found in a red-figured amphora in 330–320 BC, which depicts a flowering plant growing in a naiskos (Toledo Museum of Art, no. 1977.46; A. D. Trendall and Alexander Cambitoglou, The Red-figured Vases of Apulia, vol. 2, Oxford: Clarendon Press, 1982, p. 868, pl. 328). Extensive study is required to elucidate how the cohesion of Hellenistic plant motifs and Indian lotus originated – influences of Hellenistic and Roman art spread throughout the Silk Roads – and which cultures started to use them in silk weaving.

Maria Ludovica Rosati
Turin

Textiles patterns on the move: looking at the iconographical exchanges along the Silk Route in the pre-modern period as cultural processes

The circulation of textiles in the pre-Modern Eurasian Continent had a vast diffusion of some iconographic techniques, through time and space as a consequence. The silk medium was not the only typology of objects travelling on the ancient Eurasian routes, but it definitely benefited from a very high degree of mobility – the precious textiles often acted as a go-between for the migration of some techniques from a place to another and through them it is possible to explore the phenomenon of the exchange of patterns.[1]

At first glance the results could seem univocal, leading to the appearance of a motif far away from its original source; however, the dynamics defining such exchanges can be quite different in their reasons and developments. Moreover, the sheer circulation of objects could not be a sufficient explanation to justify the iconographic migrations.

What happens, when a foreign pattern is adopted in another context and, above all, why does it happen? Trying to answer these questions, this paper presents three cases of iconographic exchanges among Eurasian civilisations in order to analyse the variety of cultural processes connected with the transfers of patterns and their absolutely not-linear paths.

The first case of Eurasian exchange concerns the *feng huang*, when the iconography of the Chinese mythical bird appeared on the Italian silks of the late

[1] For the role of portable objects in intercultural exchanges: Hoffmann (2001: 17–50).

Middle Ages.[2] This example represents a typical case of pattern migration from East to West through the textile medium, as the Italian large scale adoption of the foreign motifs was linked to the arrival in Europe of the so-called *panni tartarici*, the luxury silks produced in many Asian centres from the Mongol Empire to Mamluk Egypt between the second half of the 13th and the 14th centuries.

It is well known how deep the impact of *panni tartarici* on the Italian silk manufactures was.[3] Here it will be enough to remember that these processes of imitation and elaboration of Asian prototypes can be ascribed to two main general reasons. On the one hand, the historical high status of exotic silks within the European concept of luxury led to a conspicuous demand for local textiles that could resemble oriental artefacts, thus shaping Western taste. On the other hand, the ornamental techniques of *panni tartarici* were perfectly in tune with European art tendencies, aiming to explore the natural world in a new way, so that Italian weavers realised a sort of reshaping process of the oriental patterns, progressively transforming them into unusual and fresh Gothic forms.

In this complex interaction between Asian models and European derivations, the *feng huang* was certainly one of the most fruitful stimuli and its iconography, more or less faithfully imitated, flooded Italian silks. Looking at the Mongol, Ilkhanid, Mamluk, and Italian textiles, we can find similar birds with long animated tails, composed of thin, sinuous ribbon-feathers, and with a rich plumage surrounding their heads (ill. 1). Even the flying postures are comparable: at times the *feng huang* is represented with a long neck in a C-torsion under the body; otherwise the body is seen from behind with the head turned in profile.[4]

To understand the fortune of this pattern and the cultural process leading to the *feng huang*'s adoption, however, it is necessary to take a step back.

Since the Ancient World some myths regarding supernatural birds had existed even in the Mediterranean tradition as a part of a more general symbolism of positive, solar, winged creatures, widespread across Eurasia. The myth of the phoenix represents the specific depiction of this archetype within the Greek-Roman imagery

---

[2] For the myth and the iconography of the Chinese *feng huang*: Rawson (1984: 99–105); Hargett (1989: 235–262); Diény (1989: 1–13); Zambon Grossato (2004: 141–162).

[3] For the *panni tartarici* and their impact in Europe: Wardwell (1988–1989: 95–173); Rosati (2010a: 58–88); Rosati (2010b: 40–63) with previous bibliography.

[4] Compare, for example, a Central Asian lampas of the late 13th century or the beginning of the 14th (New York, Metropolitan Museum of Art, inv. 1973.269) and an Italian lampas of the 14th century (Florence, Museo Nazionale del Bargello, inv. 2297C), published in When Silk was Gold (1997: cat. no. 39, 148–150) and Suriano Carboni (1999: 53–55); see also a *panno tartarico* of the end of the 13th century in the Cleveland Museum of Art (inv. 1991.5a–b), in When Silk was Gold (1997: cat. no. 41, 152), and a 14th century Italian lampas of the Kunstgewerbe Museum in Berlin (inv. W 1962.90), in Devoti (1974: 34).

and its features were defined quite early by classical authors such as Herodotus, Pliny and Tacitus. Later, reading the myth in a Christian moral and allegorical key, Isidore of Siville, Lactantius and others guaranteed its transmission to the European knowledge of the Middle Ages, when the phoenix appeared in the encyclopaedic tradition, in some liturgical texts and, above all, in the bestiary genre.[5]

Ill. 1. Detail of a silk weft-patterned lampas, Italy, middle of the 14th century (London, Victoria and Albert Museum, inv. 7084.1860)

Summarising the most common aspects of the Western myth, the phoenix is described as a solar, celestial bird coming from an undefined East. It is the unique exemplar of its species and lives alone for many centuries. When the phoenix feels its end approaching, it prepares a funeral pile with many kinds of aromatic wood. The bird dies among the flames and immediately rises again. Regarding its appearance, the beauty of the phoenix is incomparable. Its plumage is purple and gold with iridescent hues; the long tail with multi-coloured streaks and spots resembles the peacock's and some gorgeous feathers (a bunch, or, more frequently, a crest with a sunburst pattern) adorn its head like a crown.[6]

It is worth noting that the Western characterisation of the phoenix, however, belongs more to the textual rather than the visual tradition. The written sources are manifold and detailed, but they do not correspond to an equally

---

[5] For the myth of the phoenix: Van den Broek (1972); Zambon Grossato (2004: 15–42); Basile (2004).

[6] Among the most suggestive descriptions of the phoenix there are: Herodotus, *Historiae*, II, 3; Pliny the Elder, *Historia Naturalis*, X, 2; Tacitus, *Annales*, VI, 28; Solinus, *Collectanea Rerum Memorabilium*, XXXIII, 11–15, Lactantius, *Carmen de Ave Phoenice*, vv. 125–150.

Ill. 2.
Fragment of a mosaic from the ancient St. Peter's Basilica in Rome, 12th–13th centuries (Rome, Palazzo Braschi – Museo di Roma)

Ill. 3.
The Phoenix, illumination from a Bestiary, Northern or Central England, 1st quarter of the 13th century (London, British Library, ms. Royal 12, CIIX, fol. 49v)

strong iconography. Although in the Ancient World we can find some phoenix illustrations that tried to render its features (ill. 2), a sort of 'iconographical emptiness' took place during the Middle Ages. Confronted with the problem of portraying the phoenix, artists seemed to prefer depicting some topical events of the creature's life, like the burning funeral pile, quite evocative of the bird, but not requiring its specific representation. When artists tried to translate its appearance into pictures, the results were often poor and inadequate, as in a British illumination of the 13th century (ill. 3), where the phoenix resembles a roast chicken more than the quintessence of beauty.

So it is possible to suppose that the exotic *feng huang* particularly struck the imagination of Italian weavers because its form could remind them of the mythical bird of the Western tradition and it could suggest a worthy way to finally render the supernatural and elegant appearance of the phoenix. Not only could the shiny and rich plumage of the Chinese creature recall the phoenix, but also the blossomed branch carried in its beak could be read as the aromatic wood of the funeral pile. The fact that this bird appeared on Asian silks also evoked the Eastern provenance of the phoenix, indirectly justifying the superimposition of these animals. If my argument holds water, it is also possible to explain the lesser fortune of other oriental patterns in Italian silks, though they were equally present in Asian prototypes. Maybe they could recall some fabulous creatures, such as the dragon, not only already existing in the Western knowledge, but also characterised within the European visual repertoire by a strong and vital iconographical tradition. In other words, owing to a sort of 'lack of space', their adoption was unnecessary, or better, not so necessary.

Focusing on the cultural process related to *feng huang*'s migration, it could be defined as a form of 'semantic expropriation' or 'appropriation through familiarisation', that is, a foreign pattern was adopted in a new context in order to express a concept belonging to the receiving culture.[7] Even if many aspects of the Far-Eastern myth are very close to the Mediterranean one, accepting the *feng huang*'s iconography it is not a matter of recognising the similarity between these two legends. On the contrary it is plausible that, while imitating it, Italian weavers knew nothing of the Chinese symbol. Therefore, in this case, form and content had travelled separately and the deep significance of the *feng huang* seems to have been lost, at least partially, through the pattern's transfer.

The situation appears fairly different in the next pattern: the riding archer. I have chosen a specific form of the Sasanian royal hunt theme, where the rider is represented while turning back and drawing the bow string, as depicted in some Sasanian silver vessels.[8]

This pattern travelled for a long time across Eurasia through a sort of transcultural network starting from the Sasanian centre. In the West, the riding archer

---

[7] For the process of appropriation: Nelson (2003: 160–173); Ashley Plesch (2002: 1–15).

[8] For the Sasanian vessels with hunting scenes and for examples of the riding archer, turning back and drawing the bow string: Harper (1981: 40–98, pl. 8, 10, 14, 18, 19, 37). For the significance of this iconography as a kingship symbol in the Sasanian context: Bivar (2006: 9–11).

appeared in Coptic textiles and Byzantine productions; going eastwards the motif moved from Tang China to Japan.[9] Everywhere, its formal adoption involved a conscious appropriation of the meanings carried by the image. In fact it was always seen as a symbol of power, the emblem of the kingship, fighting and overcoming enemies.

This cultural elaboration, developed in the Sasanian ambit, kept a strong connection with its visual expression. Moreover, the fact that this pattern was often depicted on clothes made the symbol and content wearable, in the literal meaning of the word; so that the transfer's strength was related to an emulation process, implying a clear competitive intent. Displaying this pattern meant affirming one's own superiority before other competitors sharing the same set of visual displays of authority.[10]

Certainly this process could have been facilitated by the pre-existence in every cultural ambit involved in the exchanges of some already meaningful images, connectable with the horseman, hunter and archer concept and, unlike the phoenix, with a strong visual tradition.[11] Think of the equestrian triumph or hunting scenes in the Mediterranean tradition and their heritage in late ancient textiles. Or take the case of the celestial horses in Chinese imagery and the numerous hunter-knight representations since the Han dynasty. Consequently, different contributions and a complex semantic stratification can be seen behind the transcultural iconography of the royal riding archer and its construction in a new global dimension.

Looking at the weapons and posture of the rider, we could also ask which role the nomadic Steppes' tradition played in its formal definition. Before the birth and affirmation of the Sasanian iconography, in fact, the image of the hunter-warrior on horseback with a bow and arrow already belonged to the Eurasian repertoire and precisely this fighting technique has been recognised as typical at least since the 8th century BC of the ancient Iranian nomads, especially the Scythians.[12]

---

9 As examples of the Coptic textiles see an Egyptian fragment of tapestry of the 5th–6th centuries and a shin-pad of the early 7th century, both in the Musée des Tissus of Lyon (inv. 25520/31 and inv. 28.928): Blazy (2001: 21, 40–41). In the Byzantine ambit this pattern appears in the cloth from the tomb of St. Emidius of the Diocesan Museum of Ascoli Piceno, a silk samite of the 8th–9th centuries produced in a Syrian workshop: Lucca e l'Europa (2010: 164–166). For Far-Eastern examples see a Tang samite fragment of the 7th–8th centuries in the Abegg-Stiftung of Riggisberg (inv. 5226), in Otavsky Wardwell (2011: 24–27), or the so-called *Four Celestial Guardians Brocade* of the 7th–8th centuries from the Horyū-ji Temple (Nara), in Hayashi (1975: 126–128) and Kazuko (2006: 155–173).

10 For the adoption of this pattern and other motifs of Sasanian origin in the Byzantine silks as emulation and competitive process: Walker (2012: 23–37); Canepa (2014: 4–11).

11 For the theme of the hunt in a Eurasian perspective: Allsen (2006).

12 See, for instance, a slit woven woollen tapestry with an archer on a mythological creature (Central Asia, ca. 8 BC–234 AD), probably from Hanpul (Xinjiang), now kept in the Abegg-Stiftung, Riggisberg (inv. 5138): Baumer (2014: 140, fig. 109). For the military technique known as 'Parthian shot': Rostovtzeff (1943: 174–187); Ivantchik (2008: 177–190).

Ill. 4.
Fragment of a printed linen tabby (maybe a curtain) from the Sion Valley, western Alpine manufacture (Piedmont or Savoy), late 14th century (Zurich, Landesmuseum, inv. AG-2380)

It is interesting that this so-called nomadic component in the long life of the royal hunter pattern can also rise again with a self-contained meaning and it can produce an autonomous deviation from the significance linked with regal iconography. In the mid-thirteenth century, when the Mongol expansion was threatening the eastern boundaries of Europe, the Tartars' excellence in riding and their archery skills became proverbial in Western imagery, stimulating the creation of some iconographies, soon canonised to represent the warrior coming from the East. It is also possible that it was just this channel that allowed the recovery of the more ancient riding archer pattern, used now with a different meaning.

We can find, for example, an image very close to the traditional hunter with bow turning back in a printed linen textile of the end of the 14th century, made in the western Alpine area (ill. 4).[13] Stories of Oedipus and chivalry scenes are represented on it and our pattern appears in a picture of a battle between knights (probably from Europe) and exotic warriors with turbans. Here a useful interpretative key of this presence could be the Focillon concept of *survivance*, considered as the last phase of the appropriation process, when the original meaning of external forms has been totally forgotten in favour of unusual contents related with the new context.[14]

The concept of survival leads to the last case of pattern exchanges – a textile motif, which, in my opinion, is a real puzzle and, somehow, reminds us of the different directions followed by images on the Silk Road, not only from East to West,

---

[13] The artefact is composed of two pieces, a bigger one preserved in the Historisches Museum of Basel (inv. 1879.48) and another smaller kept in the Landesmuseum of Zurich (inv. AG-2380). This object, a curtain or a tablecloth, comes from the Sion Valley (Suisse), where it was presumably part of the furniture in an aristocratic residence. The represented clothes recall the fashion of the years 1360–1370 and there are some similarities with the illustrations of the Veneto and Lombard chivalry romances of the last quarter of the 14th century: Castronovo (2002: 227–228).

[14] Focillon (1941: 1–23).

Ill. 5. Printed silk tabby, Western Xia Dynasty (Tangut reign), 11th–12th centuries (Ningxia Hui Autonomous Region Museum)

but also from the Mediterranean area to China.

This pattern is represented on a printed silken tabby, made in the 11th or 12th centuries in the Tangut Xi Xia state, the reign between Tibet and the North-Western Chinese boundaries (ill. 5).[15] The general structure of decoration recalls pearl-roundel Tang silks, in turn derived from Sasanian and Central Asian patterns.[16] However, a very unusual motif appears among these frames: a naked child with a sinuous branch that, at first glance, recalls more the Hellenistic tradition of *putti* and cupids than the contemporary Song iconography of children playing between peonies and foliage.[17]

This strange pattern caught my attention, raising many questions. Is it a real Hellenistic *putto* or does it only look like one, belonging, instead, to a different set of images and contents? Moreover, if it is a Hellenistic motif, how could it appear on a Tangut silk from the 11th–12th centuries? Finally, is it right to read this pattern as a survival, or should we refer to another cultural process to justify its presence?

Since the Central Asia Greek-Bactrian reigns, some elements of the Mediterranean tradition had travelled eastwards merging with local expressions and through the same routes some Western artefacts also reached the East.[18] Naked Hellenistic masculine figures appeared not only in Central Asian objects, but also in some Tang

---

[15] The piece was excavated in 1986 from the Twin Pagodas in Baisikou (Yinchuan, Ningxia). For its technical analysis: Kuhn Zhao (2012: 302–303).

[16] See for instance Kuhn Zhao (2012: 211 and 213, figs. 5.3 and 5.6) and Krahl (1998: 59–63).

[17] For the typical Song iconography: Krahl (1994: 238, nn. 427–428); Krahl (1998: 64, fig. 19); Kuhn Zhao (2012: 319, fig. 6.58).

[18] As an example see a Roman silver plate from the 2th–3th centuries AD with Dionysian scenes, excavated in Gansu province where it probable arrived around the 6th–7th century thanks to the Sogdian mediation: Cina (2008: 183 and 288, cat. no. 67).

productions.[19] However, it seems necessary to find at least another step for our Tangut *putto*, as the temporal distance between this evidence and ancient and late antique examples is still too wide.

More clues could be provided by a closer observation of the motif and the consideration of the identity of Tangut producers, a semi-nomadic people of Tibetan-Burmese origin, arrived from North-Western Sichuan at the end of the 7th century and converted to Buddhism by the 10th–11th centuries.[20] Looking at the textile, we can note the unusual and non-Chinese children's hairstyles with three round shapes, maybe ornaments or chignons with red ribbons. It is comparable with some Tangut Buddhist painting of the 12th century from Khara Khoto, representing the *Amithābha* paradise (ill. 6). Here the re-born souls figure as naked children with the typical Tangut hairstyle (*tufa*): a shaved head with only some hair locks in buns or free.[21]

Ill. 6. The re-born souls of the righteous as children on the lotus in the *Amithābha* paradise. Detail of a painted cotton tanka from Khara Kotho, Tangut, early 13th century (St. Petersburg The State Hermitage Museum, inv. X-2349)

Among other previous visual evidences of this Buddhist heaven, there is a 9th century painting on silk from Dunhuang that shows the souls in the shape of children wearing a sort of short coat, similar to the one on the Tangut textile.[22] Another step back leads us to the temple-caves of Yungang in Shanxi where, in the second half of the 5th century, the *apsaras*, the aerial minor divinities of the Buddhist pantheon were carved as naked creatures in attitudes close to the Tangut motif.[23]

The reference to Gandhara art becomes inevitable, as it was one of the strongest ambits in reshaping Hellenistic forms and one of the most important vehicles

---

19 Think of the fighting naked *putti* represented on the fabric of the 3th–4th centuries AD of the so-called Yingpan Man, the mummy found in 1995 in the grave M15 of Yingapan (Xinjiang province): Hansen (2012: 40–41); Barber (2014: 38); Zhao (2014: 55–57) all with previous bibliography. See also a Tang pilgrim flask of the early 8th century with a dancing Hellenistic *putto* among branches, now in the Royal Ontario Museum of Toronto: Beurdeley (1985: 155, fig. 160).

20 On the Tangut Empire: Lost Empire (1993: 49–58).

21 Lost Empire (1993: 77–80, 89–91, 182–185, 194–195).

22 Paris, Musée Guimet (inv. EO 1152), in Sérinde (1995: 329–330, cat. no. 248).

23 Watson (2003: 129–145, fig. 64).

Ill. 7. *Putti* with dog, carved slab, grey schist, Gandhara region, 1st century, Antiquarian market (John Eskenazi London)

for its long duration in Central Asia. In some carved Gandhara slabs we can find not only some images of children, clearly moulded after Hellenistic cupids and *putti*, but also bracelets and necklaces similar to the Tangut example (ill. 7).[24] Moreover, these Gandharian *putti* show some flowers in the hair that in turn could help to explain the strange round ornaments on the head of the Tangut children.

The Buddhist source, therefore, could be a useful key for reading this pattern. Nevertheless, what is even more intriguing is the fact that if we want to consider the entire textile pattern as a sort of celestial vision, we should refer not only to the Buddhist tradition, but also maybe to the Taoist one: the fruits here represented in fact seem to be peaches, a typical food of the Immortals in the Taoist heaven.[25]

Although it is not possible yet to trace the exact genesis of our *putto* pattern, nevertheless, the many sources (Chinese, Tangut, Hellenistic, Buddhist) identifiable in it make it plausible to consider it as the result of a 'hybridisation' process, a way to create new patterns and meanings by reshaping and merging different external forms.[26]

Therefore, this cultural process and the others mentioned above reflect not only the extraordinary fluidity of exchanges, but also the creative power developing from the cultural meetings that occurred seamlessly along the Silk Road.

BIBLIOGRAPHY

Allsen 2006 = Thomas T. Allsen, *The Royal Hunt in Eurasian History*, Philadelphia: University of Pennsylvania Press, 2006.

Art of Gandhara 1998 = *Art of Gandhara*, exhibition cat., John Eskenazi (ed.), London: Eskenazi Gallery, 1998.

Ashley Plesch 2002 = Kathleen M. Ashley, Véronique Plesch, "The Cultural Processes of Appropriation", *Journal of Medieval and Eraly Modern Studies*, 23/1 (2002): 1–15.

Barber 2014 = Elizabeth Wayland Barber, "More Light on the Xinjiang Textiles". In *Reconfiguring the Silk Road. New Research on East-West Exchange in Antiquity*, Victor H. Mair,

[24] See for example Art of Gandhara (1998: 19–22).

[25] See 'Peach' in Welch (2008: 55).

[26] For this cultural process and its creative strength: Kapchan Strong (1999: 239–253) and Hannerz (2000: 12–15).

Jane Hickman (eds.), Philadelphia: University of Pennsylvania Museum of Archaeology and Anthopology, 2014.

Basile 2004 = Bruno Basile, *La fenice. Da Claudiano a Tasso* (The Phoenix. From Claudian to Tasso), Rome: Carocci, 2004.

Baumer 2014 = Christoph Baumer, *The History of Central Asia*, vol 2: *The Age of the Silk Roads*, London – New York: I.B. Tauris, 2014.

Beurdeley 1985 = Cécile Beurdeley, *Sur les Routes de la Soie. Le grand voyage des objects d'art* (On the Silk Roads. The Long Travel of the Artefacts), Fribourg: Seuil, 1985.

Bivar 2006 = Adrian David Huge Bivar, "Sasanian Iconography on Textiles and Seals". In *Central Asian Textiles and Their Contexts in the Early Middle Ages*, Regula Schorta (ed.), Riggisberger Berichte 9, Riggisberg: Abegg-Stiftung, 2006: 9–21.

Blazy 2001 = Guy Blazy *et al.*, *Musée des Tissus de Lyon. Guide des collections* (Musée des Tissus of Lyon. Collections Guide), Lyon: Editions Lyonnaisses d'art et d'Histoire 2001.

Canepa 2014 = Matthew P. Canepa, "Textiles and Elite Tastes between the Mediterranean, Iran and Asia at the End of Antiquity". In *Global Textiles Encounters*, Marie-Louise Nosch, Zhao Feng, Lotika Varadarajan (eds.), Oxford – Philadelphia: Oxbow Books, 2014, pp. 1–14.

Castronovo 2002 = Simonetta Castronovo, "Il mondo cavalleresco. L'Italia nord-occidentale" (The Chivalry World. Northern-Western Italy). In *Il Gotico nelle Alpi: 1350–1450* (Gothic in the Alpes: 1350–1450), Enrico Castelnuovo, Francesca de Gramatica (eds.), exhibition cat., Trento: Castello del Buonconsiglio, 2002, pp. 224–237.

Cina 2008 = *Cina. Alla corte degli Imperatori. Capolavori mai visti dalla tradizione Han all'eleganza Tang (25–907)* (China. At the Imperial Court. Never seen Masterpieces from the Han Tradition to the Tang Elegance), Sabrina Rastelli (ed.), exhibition cat., Florence: Palazzo Strozzi, 2008, Milano: Skira, 2008.

Devoti 1974 = Donata Devoti, *L'arte del tessuto in Europa* (Textile Art in Europe), Milan: Bramante, 1974.

Diény 1989 = Jean-Pierre Diény, "Le Fenghuang et le Phénix" (Fenghuang and Phoenix), *Cahiers d'Extrême-Asie* (Quarterly of Far East), 5 (1989), pp. 1–13.

Focillon 1941 = Henri Focillon, "Préhistoire et Moyen Âge" (Prehistory and Middle Ages), *Dumbarton Oaks Papers*, 1 (1941), pp. 1–23.

Hannerz 2000 = Ulf Hannerz, "Flows, Boundaries and Hybrids: Keywords in Transnational Anthropology", *Working Paper Series. University of Oxford. Transnational Communities Program*, (2000), pp. 1–25, http://www.transcomm.ox.ac.uk/working%20papers/hannerz.pdf (entry: 30.11.2015).

Hansen 2012 = Valerie Hansen, *The Silk Road. A New History*, New York: Oxford University Press, 2012.

Hargett 1989 = James Hargett, "Playing Second Fiddle: The Luan-Bird in Early and Medieval Chinese Literature", *T'oung Pao*, 75/4–5 (1989), pp. 235–262.

Harper 1981 = Prudence Oliver Harper, *Silver Vessels of the Sasanian Period*, vol. 1: *Royal Imagery*, New York: Metropolitan Museum of Art, 1981.

Hayashi 1975 = Ryoichi Hayashi, *The Silk Road and the Shoso-in*, New York–Tokyo: Weatherhill/Heibonsha, 1975.

Hoffmann 2001 = Eva Hoffmann, "Pathways of Portability: Islamic and Christian Interchange from Tenth to Twelfth Century", *Art History*, 24/1 (2001), pp. 17–50.

Kapchan Strong 1999 = Deborah A. Kapchan, Pauline Turner Strong, "Theorizing the Hybrid", *The Journal of American Folklore*, 112/115 (1999), pp. 239–253.

Kazuko 2006 = Yokohari Kazuko, "The Hōryū-ji Lion-hunting Silk and Related Silks", in *Central Asian Textiles and Their Contexts in the Early Middle Ages*, Regula Schorta (ed.), Riggisberger Berichte 9, Riggisberg: Abegg-Stiftung, 2006, pp. 155–173.

Krahl 1994 = Regina Krahl, *Chinese Ceramics from the Meiyintang Collection*, 2 voll., London: Azimut, 1994.

Krahl 1998 = Regina Krahl, "Designs on Early Chinese Textiles", *Chinese and Central Asian Textiles: Selected Articles from Orientations 1983–1997*, Hong Kong 1998, pp. 56–65.

Kuhn Zhao 2012 = Dieter Kuhn, Feng Zhao (eds.), *Chinese Silks*, New Haven – London: Yale University Press, 2012.

Ivantchik 2008 = Askold Ivantchik, "Le *Parthian Shot* cinquante ans après Rostovtzeff" (The *Parthian Shot* Fifty Years after Rostovtzeff), in: *Michel Ivanovtich Rostovtzeff*, Jean Andreau, Wladimir Berelowitch (eds.), Bari: Edipuglia, 2008, pp. 177–190.

Lost Empire 1993 = *Lost Empire of the Silk Road. Buddhist Art from Khara Khoto*, Mikhail Piotrovskji (ed.), exhibition cat., Lugano: Thyssen Bornemisza Foundation, Milan: Electa, 1993.

Lucca e l'Europa 2010 = *Lucca e L'Europa. Un'idea di Medioevo, V–XI secolo* (Lucca and Europe. An Idea of Middle Ages, 5th–10th centuries), Clara Baracchini, Antonino Caleca, Marco Collareta, Gigetta Dalli Regoli, Maria Teresa Filieri (eds.), exhibition cat., Lucca: Fondazione Ragghianti, 2010.

Nelson 2003 = Robert S. Nelson, "Appropriation". In *Critical Terms for Art History*, Robert S. Nelson, Richard Shiff (eds.), Chicago: The University of Chicago Press, 2003 (2nd ed.), pp. 160–173.

Otavsky Wardwell 2011 = Karel Otavsky, Anne E. Wardwell, *Mittelalterliche Textilien II. Zwischen Europa und China* (Middle Ages Textiles II. Between Europe and China), Riggisberg: Abegg-Stiftung, 2011.

Rawson 1984 = Jessica Rawson, *Chinese Ornament: The Lotus and the Dragon*, London: British Museum Publications, 1984, pp. 12–24.

Rosati 2010a = Maria Ludovica Rosati, "Migrazioni tecnologiche e interazioni culturali. La diffusione dei tessuti orientali nell'Europa del XIII e del XIV secolo" (Technological Migrations and Cultural Interactions. The Diffusion of the Oriental Textiles in the 13th–14th Centuries Europe), *OADI. Rivista dell'Osservatorio per le Arti Decorative in Italia* (OADI. Journal of the Observatory for Decorative Arts in Italy), 1/1 (2010), pp. 58–88.

Rosati 2010b = Maria Ludovica Rosati, "Migrazioni tecnologiche e interazioni culturali. Chinoiserie ed esotismo nell'arte tessile italiana del XIII e del XIV secolo" (Technological Migrations and Cultural Interactions. Chinoiserie and Exoticism in the Italian Textiles of the 13th and 14th Centuries), *OADI. Rivista dell'Osservatorio per le Arti Decorative in Italia* (OADI. Journal of the Observatory for Decorative Arts in Italy), 1/2 (2010), pp. 40–63.

Rostovtzeff 1943 = Michel I. Rostovtzeff, "The Parthian Shot", *American Journal of Archaeology*, 47/2 (1943), pp. 174–187.

Sérinde 1995 = *Sérinde, terre de Bouddha. Dix siècles d'art sur la Route de la Soie* (Serinde, Lands of Buddha. Ten Centuries of Art along the Silk Road), Monique Cohen, Jacques Giès (eds.), exhibition cat., Paris: Galeries Nationales du Grand Palais, 1995–1996, Paris: Réunion des Musées Nationaux, 1995.

Suriano Carboni 1999 = Carlo Maria Suriano, Stefano Carboni, *La seta islamica. Temi ed influenze culturali* (Islamic Silk. Themes and Cultural Influences), Florence: S.P.E.S., 1999.

Van den Broek 1972 = Roelof van den Broek, The Myth of the Phoenix According to Classical and Early Christian Tradition, Leiden: Brill, 1972.

Walker 2012 = Alicia Walker, The Emperor and the World. Exotic Elements and the Imagining of Middle Byzantine Imperial Power, Ninth to Thirteenth Centuries CE, New York: Cambridge University Press, 2012.

Wardwell 1988–1989 = Anne E. Wardwell, "Panni Tartarici. Eastern Islamic Silk Woven with Gold and Silver (13th and 14th Centuries)", *Islamic Art: An Annual Dedicated to the Art and Culture of the Muslim World,* 3 (1988–1989), pp. 95–173.

Watson 2003 = William Watson, *L'arte della Cina. Nuova edizione riveduta e accresciuta* (Chinese Art. New Revised and Increased Edition), Marie-Catherine Rey (ed.), Milano: Garzanti, 2003.

Welch 2008 = Patricia Welch, *Chinese Art: A Guide To Motifs and Visual Imagery*, Singapore: Tuttle Publishing, 2008.

When Silk was Gold 1997 = *When Silk was Gold. Central Asian and Chinese Textiles*, James c.Y. Watt, Anne E. Wardwell (eds.), exhibition cat., New York: The Metropolitan Museum of Art, 1997.

Zambon Grossato 2004 = Francesco Zambon, Alessandro Grossato, *Il mito della fenice in Oriente e in Occidente* (The Myth of the Phoenix in the East and the West), Marsilio, Venice 2004.

Zhao 2014 = Feng Zhao, "The Development of Pattern Weaving Technology through Textile Exchange along the Silk Road". In *Global Textiles Encounters*, Marie-Louise Nosch, Zhao Feng, Lotika Varadarajan (eds.), Oxford – Philadelphia: Oxbow Books, 2014, pp. 49–64.

Credits

1. Devoti (1974: 40)
2. Van den Broek (1972: pl. I)
3. Public Domain Mark from http://www.bl.uk/catalogues/illuminatedmanuscripts
4. © Landesmuseum Zurich
5. Kuhn Zhao (2012: fig. 6.42, p. 303)
6. Lost Empire (1993: 194, cat. no. 44)
7. Art of Gandhara (1998: 19)

Beata Biedrońska-Słota
Polish Institute of World Art Studies

The cross-cultural role of textiles exemplified by textiles with Arabic inscriptions and some other motifs[1]

Textiles have often been treated as cross-cultural phenomena in studies on the transmission of art forms between cultures. Elegant silk textiles, imported to Europe from the East since the Early Mediaeval times, were a source of inspiration and innovative stylistic concepts. Eastern textiles in Europe became a sign of wealth; they distinguished their possessors as members of the elites, in court and in church. The textiles imported from the Near and Middle East to Europe inspired imitations manufactured in European workshops, mainly in Italy and in Spain. As a result, among the rich patterns that contribute to the artistic expression of Mediaeval European textiles, we can see many elements imported from oriental ornaments, transmitted by diffusion and already adopted in Europe in the Early Middle Ages. In this way the patterns and their elements acquired from the East enriched various domains of European art.

The migration of ornamental motifs mediated by textiles has been already studied by some authors. It was A. Riegl who noticed that textiles were a source of inspiration for artists in areas very distant from the areas of their production.[2] Easy for transfer over large distances, textiles always accompanied people. It is for

---

[1] The papers were prepared in connection with the Interdisciplinary study of a set of 192 items of medieval liturgical vestments from the Saint Mary Church in Gdansk, now stored in the National Museum in Gdansk, with a particular focus on technology and technical research. Funded by NCN (No 13/09/B/HS2/1/01197), briefly The TREASURE of MEDIEVAL VESTMENTS in Gdansk project led by the Chair of Conservation and Restoration of the Historic Textiles of Fine Arts Academy in Warsaw and the National Museum in Gdansk.

[2] Riegl (1891); Recently this topic was noticed and studied by Hansen (2012).

this reason why today they are a rich source of information on contacts, mutual inspirations and relations. Careful analysis of the motifs used in textile decoration reveals how motifs may acquire new meanings when transferred to a new context.[3]

The main land trade route from the Far East, first of all China, to Europe, through the countries of the Middle and Near East, was the Silk Road. It was by this route that various goods, including textiles, arrived in the countries of the Mediterranean. The history of the Silk Road is long and involves contact between various countries along the route. For example, textiles produced in China could be purchased in Iran as well as in Europe. By this route merchants brought various goods to Europe in various periods of history, depending on the current politics, economical relationships, financial resources and interests of the European oligarchs. So in times of the Mongolian Ilkhanate textiles from Central Asia came to Europe by the routes controlled by the Mongols. It should be noted that apart from the Silk Road, many textiles arrived from the East to Venice by sea.

For an art historian perhaps the most interesting period of trade between Europe and the East are the Middle Ages. An analysis of patterns used in textile decoration reveals that the impact of the Orient on European art was then much greater than had been generally accepted. This is confirmed by silk textiles preserved in European collections, those imported from the East and those produced in European workshops and decorated with Eastern patterns. In the Middle Ages, the production of silk textiles using the oriental technique and patterns was undertaken by Lucca and later by other Italian workshops. Several workshops producing silk textiles had already been set up there earlier, during the Arab rule in Spain. Their history is being increasingly studied using both, Latin and Arabian sources.

One result of these close intercultural relationships is that it is often difficult to distinguish the textiles made in Europe from those made in Asia in the Late Middle Ages. We may quote here an example from the introduction to an inventory written in Rome in 1311: "a tunic made of white Tartarian or Luccan matter, with an ornament in horizontal stripes of red silk and gold."[4]

The relations between the East and West may be studied perfectly by examining textiles preserved in Polish collections. They may be grouped into several assemblages on the grounds of the patterns used in their designs.[5] The most interesting group are the textiles with Arabic inscriptions. They include original textiles with Arabic inscriptions imported from the East and their imitations produced in Italy.

---

[3] Ganzhorn (1998).

[4] Wardwell (1989: 136).

[5] Bochnak (1968: 154–155); Biedrońska-Słotowa (1994: 13–19); Biedrońska-Słotowa (1996: 248–254).

Ill. 1. Chasuble, National Museum in Gdansk, inv. no. MNG 238 (Foto: Monika Stachurska)

Ill. 2. Chasuble, National Museum in Gdansk, inv. no. MNG 239 (Foto: Monika Stachurska)

They demonstrate most clearly the relations between the original Arabic textiles with inscriptions and their imitations from Italy.

Liturgical vestments decorated with Arabic inscriptions are present in the collection of the National Museum in Gdansk – a set comprising two chasubles, nr MNG 238 (ill. 1)[6] and MNG 239 (ill. 2),[7] two dalmatics nr MNG 275, 276 (ills. 3–4)[8] and a cope MNG 232 (ill. 5).[9] All are sewn from textiles with patterns almost identical but differing in details. Generally the patterns consist of stripes with rhythmically changing widths and background colours, decorated successively as follows: 1) wider stripes filled with a continuous inscription repeating

6 Hinz (1863: 33); Karabacek (1870: 141–147); Falke (1913, II: 38, fig. 31 and 308, abb. 350); Mannowsky (1929: 15, no. 30); Mannowsky (1930–33,2: 3–4, cat. 30, tabl. 46); Żelewska (1964: 113, 86); Żelewska (1966: 1, fig. 2); Biedrońska-Słotowa (ed. 1992, cat. no. I/54, fig. 26).

7 Karabacek (1870: 141–147); Lessing (1900, pl. 1203); Żarnowiecki (1915: 68, 70–71, fig. 29); Mannowsky (1929); Mannowsky (1930–33, 2: 3-4, cat. 33, tabl. 49); Gotische Paramente und Bildwerke (1934: 14); Aus dem Danziger Paramentenschatz (1958: 11); Biedrońska-Słotowa (1992, cat. no. I/55, fig. 27).

8 Karabacek (1870, 5: 4); Hinz (1863: 57); Mannowsky (1930–33, cat.113, 114, tabl. 124, 125).

9 Mannowsky (1930–33, cat.17, tabl. 22).

Ill. 3.
Dalmatic, National Museum in Gdansk,
inv. no. MNG 275
(Foto: Monika Stachurska)

Ill. 4.
Dalmatic, National Museum in Gdansk,
inv. no. MNG 276
(Foto: Monika Stachurska)

the phrase *as-sultan al–alim* (Sultan the Knower, Wisest); 2) stripes of uniform width filled with two rhythmically alternating motifs: medallions with a lotus blossom and rosettes with a geometrical ornament. Rhythmically interspersed between them are pairs of antithetic birds (peacocks) alternating with

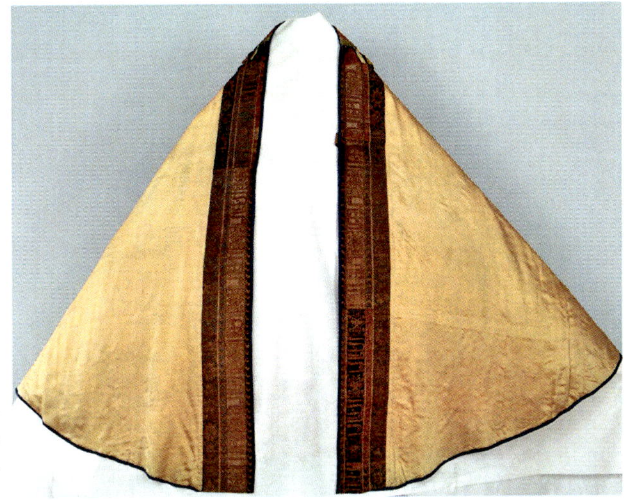

Ill. 5.
Cope, National Museum in Gdansk, inv. no. MNG 232 (Foto: Monika Stachurska)

Ill. 6. Fragments of the chasuble, National Museum in Gdansk, inv. no. NMG 238 (Foto: B. Biedrońska-Słotowa)

Ill. 7. Fragments of the chasuble, National Museum in Gdansk, inv. no. NMG 238 (Foto: B. Biedrońska-Słotowa)

antithetically arranged animal silhouettes (ill. 6); 3) narrow stripes filled with silhouettes of running dogs in collars and of fawns, separated by closed crescents (ill. 7). Our study revealed that the textiles were made in the Mongol Ilkhanate in northern Persia, during the first half of the 14th century, when the Mongol Empire ruled there.[10] They were made by weavers brought from China, using designs by Persian artists and in accordance with the Chinese technique. They are perhaps the best example of an artistic exchange and the diffusion of forms and techniques as a consequence of the political decisions of a ruler. Informa-

---

[10] Kendrick (1924: 67, cat. 997, pl. XXII); Wardwell (1989: 95–173, abb. 42); Wilckens (1991: fig. 98); Wilckens (1992: cat. 82–84); Legacy (2003: cat. no. 75, fig. 196. I); Ritter (2010: 105–135).

tion on the transfers of artists and weaving techniques is provided by historical sources and travel journals. The Mongols settled Persian artists in the southern extremes of their territory. The artists originated mostly from Khorasan – e.g. from Herat, famous for its golden and silver textiles and from Turkestan, e.g. from Samarkand. The Chinese weavers sent to the same places were transferred to Central Asia with the goal of manufacturing for the Mongols according to the Chinese technique.

The described textiles may be included in the group of luxury silk textiles weaved with a large amount of golden threads. The Mongols were interested in their production for many reasons. Many facts suggest that the textiles, because of their high artistic value, were considered by the Mongols as the prime form of artistic expression. This is why the textiles were placed higher than painting and sculpture in the hierarchy of Mongol art.[11] As such they were used for precious gifts, handed over as diplomatic presents as was the case when Ilkhan Teguder Ahmed, the ruler of the Mongol Ilkhanat in Persia in years 1282–1384, handed over similar textiles to the Mamluks. The textiles demonstrated the standing, prestige and political power of their owner. They could also be used in paying tributes, especially among rulers. Ilkhan Hulegu (1256–1265), for example, received from China a tribute paid partly in textiles. The high material value of the Oriental textiles often resulted in them becoming a symbolic currency and an equivalent of money.

The described textiles with Arabic inscriptions in Polish collections were purchased for St. Mary's Church in Gdansk with the aim of using them to sew liturgical vestments for the church.

The collection of liturgical vestments from St. Mary's Church in Gdansk preserved in The National Museum in Gdansk includes also vestments made from textiles from the Italian workshops, whose ornaments include motifs of Arabic script, a clear imitation of inscriptions on original Oriental textiles.

The cope (MNG/SD/228) may serve as an example (ill. 8).[12] The background consists of a monochromatic pattern, created in the damask technique, with a motif of branches with a large fan-like palmette placed in the apex and an ovate banderole with an inscription imitating Arabic script in the lower part. The motifs are placed over one another in rows. Motifs of dogs in collars and lions are placed within loops formed by the banderol; pelicans and eagles are placed between them. The cope's belt is made from a textile with a continuous pattern formed by a network of large diamonds marked by stripes filled in one half with floral twigs and in the other half with Pseudo-Kufic inscriptions. A similar motif is used in the decoration of the

[11] When the Silk was Gold (1998: 127–165).

[12] Mannowsky (1930–1933: vol. I, cat. no. 8, tabl. 13, 14).

textile used for the copes MNG/SD/229 (ill. 9).[13] In this case, the banderol with a Pseudo-Kufic inscription is placed below the motifs of antithetic animals. Yet another example is provided by the belt of a cope with Pseudo-Kufic motifs placed in medallions. A familiar phenomenon in the art of many periods and cultures, pseudo script was cultivated in Italian painting, sculpture and other crafts.

Ill. 8. Fragments of the chasuble, National Museum in Gdansk, inv. no. NMG 228 (Foto: B. Biedrońska-Słotowa)

Other motifs may also provide an illustration of the textile-mediated exchange between the West and East. A dalmatic in the collection of the Victoria and Albert Museum has a pattern composed of pelicans and dogs in collars in a style typical of European ornaments (V&A 8361-1863). The technique, however, is oriental, akin to that in the textiles produced at the time when the Mongolian Empire already dominated Iran. It is noteworthy that the production of such a rich textile required a drawloom workshop run by two artisans: a weaver who operated the workshop and created the fabric of the textile, and a drawboy to assist the weaver and raise and lower the warp. The place of origin of such workshops is not known. They could have originated simultaneously in China and in the Middle East. Their introduction lasted for a long time along the coasts of the Mediterranean Sea during the Mongolian invasion in the 13th century. The pattern, on the other hand, was borrowed by the oriental artists from the Italian one.[14]

Similar motifs also decorate the cope from the National Museum in Gdansk (MNG 228), mentioned earlier in connection with the motifs on the banderole with Pseudo-Kufic inscriptions inserted within the pattern (ill. 8). These are motifs of dogs with collars and lions. Among them, pelicans and eagles also appear rhythmically alternating in rows, brocaded with a golden thread, in a net-like

[13] Mannowsky (1930–33: vol. I, cat. no. 9, tabl. 16, 17).

[14] Wardwell (1989: 123–125).

Ill. 9.
Fragment of the cape, National Museum in Gdansk, inv. no. MNG 229 (Foto: B. Biedrońska-Słotowa)

Ill. 10.
Fragment of the cape, National Museum in Gdansk, inv. no. MNG 231 (Foto: B. Biedrońska-Słotowa)

arrangement. The cope's belt is made from a fabric with a somewhat different ornament. This is a continuous ornament consisting of a network of large diamonds delineated by stripes filled in half with floral twigs and in half with a Pseudo-Kufic inscription. Symmetrical axial motifs of pomegranate fruits and antithetic eagles, dogs and lions are placed within the network cells.

This example confirms the observations on the close artistic and technical relationships between the East and West.[15]

Another motif appearing among the ornaments on textiles is also noteworthy. This is the motif of a feathered serpent. It is present in the design of textiles produced most probably at Lukka or in Venice, from which was made the fabric of a cope from St. Mary's Church in Gdansk (MNG 231).[16] The pattern consists of a gothic crenellation in the form of a triangle delineated by a stripe with a geometrical ornament, with a finial on top; below is placed the motif of a feathered serpent; further below, in beams, a pair of angels in flight supporting a thick

---

[15] More about this dalmatic: Stanley (2004).
[16] Mannowsky (1930–33: vol. I, cat., no. 15, tabl. 21).

crescent; further below two pairs of fighting animals symmetrically arranged: a spotted predator and a herbivore (a leopard and a hind); the leopard has a green collar (ill. 10).

The motif of a feathered serpent as well as the motif of fighting animals belongs to the repertoire of Chinese art; it often appears in Persian art from ancient times, and later most frequently in the design of carpets from the 16th century. In European art it appears among the ornaments on textiles already in the 12th century on the King Roger's cope, and very frequently in Lucca in the 14th century as a kind of transfer of the design from Persian miniatures. In European art it appears in a literal interpretation and then on the textiles from the Lucca workshops.

The migration and exchange of motifs, presented here on selected examples, are especially intriguing in the case of the motifs appearing on the vestments used in liturgy of the Catholic church. Each motif, according to the Mediaeval iconographic record, had its own symbolic meaning. So finding appropriate interpretations of the feathered serpents, inscriptions in Arabic alphabet, crescents, fighting animals and other motifs is a goal for further investigation.

As mentioned earlier, the luxury oriental silk textiles were imported to the European states mainly for in order to sew vestments for state rulers and high clergy. From the European viewpoint, these textiles brought with them the tradition of splendour of the Eastern rulers and the patterns used in their ornaments were meant to represent the symbolic links with the Orient. Almost at the same time, these admirable textiles were imitated by Italian manufactures, of which the most important was the one in Lucca. This is why the textiles from Lucca mostly bear motifs borrowed from Chinese and Persian art. The studies on the exchange of motifs between the arts of the East and West along the Silk Road demonstrate how advanced was the European understanding of the East and the demand for oriental products, especially from the 12th to the 14th century – the period of the predominance of the Mongol state, whose strong development provided an impetus for the commercial exchange along the Silk Road and with European states.

BIBLIOGRAPHY

Aus dem Danziger Paramentenschatz = *Aus dem Danziger Paramentenschatz und dem Schatz der Schwarzhaupter zu Riga,* Nürnberg 1958.

Biedrońska-Słotowa 1992 = Beata Biedrońska-Słotowa (ed.*), Orient w sztuce polskiej* (Orient in the Polish art), Kraków: Muzeum Naroowe w Krakowie, 1992.

Biedrońska-Słotowa 1994 = Beata Biedrońska-Słotowa, "Early 15th Century Byzantine and Mamluk Textiles from Wawel Cathedral, Cracow", *Bulletin du CIETA* 72, 1994.

Biedrońska-Słotowa 1996 = Beata Biedrońska-Słotowa, „Bliskowschodnie tkaniny liturgiczne i ich rola w katedrze na Wawelu w czasach biskupa Zbigniewa Oleśnickiego" (Middle-Eastern canonical dresses and their role at the Wawel cathedral in the time of bishop

Zbigniew Olesnicki). In *Sztuka około 1400. Materiały sesji Stowarzyszenia Historyków Sztuki, Poznań 1995*, Warszawa 1996.

Bochnak 1968 = Adam Bochnak: "Groby królowej Jadwigi i królewicza Kazimierza Jagiellończyka w katedrze wawelskiej" (Tombs of the queen Jadwiga and the prince Casimir IV in the Wawel cathedral). In *Studia do dziejów Wawelu*, vol. III, Kraków: Ministerstwo Kultury i Sztuki, Zarząd Muzeów i Ochrony Zabytków, 1968.

Falke 1913 = Otto von Falke, *Kunstgeschichte der Seidenwebereien*, vol. II, Berlin: Ernst Wasmuth, 1913.

Gantzhorn 1998 = Volkmar Gantzhorn, *Oriental Carpets,* Köln: Taschen, 1998.

Hansen 2012 = Valerie Hansen, *Silk Road. A New History*, Oxford: Oxford University Press, 2012.

Hinz 1863 = A. Hinz, *Die Schatzkammer der Marienkirche zu Danzig* (The Treasury of the Saint Mary's church in Danzig), Danzig 1863.

Karabacek 1870 = Josef Karabacek, "Die liturgischen Gewander mit arabischen Inschriften aus der Marienkirche in Danzig" (Cannonical dresses with Arabic inscriptions from the Saint Mary's church in Danzig), *Mitteilungen des K. K. Österreichischen Museums*, V, Wien 1870.

Kendrick 1924 = Albert Frank Kendrick, *Catalogue of Muhammadan Textiles of the Medieval Period*, London: Victoria and Albert Museum, 1924.

Legacy 2003 = *The Legacy of Geenghis Khan. Courtly Art and Culture in Western Asia, 1256–1353*, exhibition cat., New York: The Metropolitan Museum of Art, 2003.

Lessing 1900 = Julius Lessing, *Die Gewebesammlung des K. Kunstgewerbemuseums,* Berlin: E. Wasmuth, 1900.

Mannowsky 1929 = Walter Mannowsky, *Kirchliche Gewänder und Stickereien aus dem Schatz der Marienkirche,* Danzig 1929.

Mannowsky 1930–33 = Walter Mannowsky, *Der Danziger Paramentenschatz*, 2, Berlin: Brandussche Verlagsbuchhandlung, 1930–33.

Riegl 1981 = Alois Riegl, *Altorientalische Teppiche*, Leipzig 1891

Ritter 2010 = Markus Ritter, "Kunst mit Botschaft: Der Gold-Seide-Stoff fur den Ilchan Abu Sa`id von Iran (Grabgewand Rudolfs IV. In Wien) – Rekonstruktion, Typus, Reprasentationsmedium", *Beitrage zur Islamischen Kunst und Archaologie*, 2, Wiesbaden: Reichert, 2010, pp. 105–135.

Stanley 2004 = Tim Stanley, *Palace and Mosque, Islamic art from the Middle East,* London: Victoria & Albert Museum, 2004.

Wardwell 1989 = Anne E. Wardwell, "Panni Tartarici: Eastern Islamic Woven with Gold and Silver (13th and 14th centuries) " *Islamic Art*, III, Genova: Bruschettini Foundation for Islamic and Asian Art, New York: Islamic Art Foundation, 1989.

When Silk Was Gold 1998 = *When Silk Was Gold. Central Asian and Chinese Textiles,* James c. Y. Watt, Anne E. Wardwell, Morris Rossabi, exhibition cat., New York: The Metropolitan Museum of Art, 1998.

Wilckens = Leonie von Wilckens, *Die Textilen Kunste von der Spätantike bis um 1500* (The textile arts from the late antiquity to 1500), Munchen: c.H. Beck, 1991.

Wilckens = Leonie von Wilckens, *Mittelalterliche Seidenstoffe* (Medieval silk fabrics), Berlin: Berlin Kunstgewerbemuseum, 1992.

Żarnowiecki 1915 = Longin Żarnowiecki, Historya tkanin jedwabnych (History of the sil textiles), Kijev: Drukarnia Polska w Kijowie, 1915.

Żelewska 1964 = Maria Żelewska, „Wystawa gdańskiego zbioru tkanin zabytkowych" (Exhibition from the Danzig collection of historic textiles). In *Muzealnictwo*, Warszawa-Poznań 1964, p. 113, Ill. 86.
Żelewska 1966 = Maria Żelewska, *Gdański zbiór tkanin średniowiecznych* (The Danzig collection of historic textiles), Gdańsk 1966.

Cemile Tuna
Istanbul Kemerburgaz University

Silk trade from Bursa to Krakow on the Silk Road

The routes that created a flow of armies, ideas, religions, trade and cultures from Asia to Europe and from Europe to Asia throughout history, became identified with the most extraordinary product known to the West and came to be known as the Silk Road. Silk has been a commodity of social status, communication and trade as well as a valuable element that spread the movement of art.

The Silk Road, starting from the Xi'an city of China, reaches Anatolia and the Mediterranean through Uzbekistan, Kashgar, Khazar (Caspian) and Iran. Introduction of Chinese silk to Middle East and Europe dates back to the Roman Empire. For over a thousand years, the Silk Road had been controlled by Turkish states. The Uighurs, Göktürks, Seljuks and Ottomans, – known as the Silk Empires – showed utmost care to keep this grand route alive. Under the security granted by the Turkish states, on an effective network of routes, composed of roads which were built during the Roman Empire and the Byzantium era, bridges, inns and caravanserais, camel caravans with valuable loads of silk, porcelain, paper, spices, jade and other precious stones, carried their cargo from East to the ports of the Mediterranean and the Black Sea and through Thrace to Europe.

Starting from the Middle Age, silk had been the most important and most precious commodity of intercontinental trade. In the 13th century, silk from China was woven into valuable textiles in the advanced ateliers of Europe and Anatolia; but after the year 1270, silk from China could not reach the markets due to political agitations in the Mongolian Empire which controlled the silk from China, and had been replaced by silk from Persia. This change of route placed Bursa, the centre of Byzantium and Seljuk silk processing and trade, and the first capital of the Ottoman Empire, as the centre of transcontinental trade between East and West.

"Around the year 1500, Bursa used to welcome five to six Persian camel caravans every year, each carrying minimum 1200 loads (about 100–200 tons) of silk worth nearly one million gold ducats each".[1] The merchants accompanying the caravans, were obligated to unload their valuable merchandise in Koza Han – built during the reign of Ottoman Sultan Bayezid II, as a trade centre commissioned by the Ottoman government, and served as the greatest silk market. Silk was only allowed to leave the Han after being documented and taxed by the officers. "During the rule of Bayezid II the Ottoman treasury earned approximately 70.000 gold ducats per year from the silk trade".[2] Bursa served not only as the capital of the Ottoman Empire, but the capital of advancements in politics and trade of that era. Tabriz, Trabzon and Aleppo; the silk transferred on these routes had always been gathered in Bursa and distributed among foreign merchants and local ateliers after being valued and sold here. "Towards the end of 15th century, there were almost a thousand weaving looms in Bursa and a significant portion of silk from East was being processed in the city".[3]

Ottoman Bursa wasn't solely the main market for Persian silk; it was also an important market for Arabian and Indian spices, medicine and dyes. These valuable commodities were transferred to Bursa through Mecca-Damascus-Aleppo, then exported to Poland and the Nordic countries through Akkerman-Lviv route, passing through the Balkans and Hungary. Ottoman and European merchants used to wait in Bursa for the international trading of goods between East and West. The Ottoman silk textiles exported to Eastern countries and Europe came to be known as "Bursa Textiles".

"Bursa was mainly dominated by its connection to the Ottoman Palace and partly depended on markets of Istanbul; however it was also an important centre of international trade".[4] In the city, which housed an active guild system, silk was processed into numerous kinds of precious textiles like velvet, *kemha*, satin. Among the main categories of silk weaving, heavy *kemha*s – weaved and adorned with gold and silver – were the most valuable.

Between the 15th and 18th centuries, Ottoman Palace had been the prime supervisor and client of the textiles processed in weaving looms of Bursa. The preference of materials, patterns, technical features and aesthetic rules to be followed exhibits the power and admiration of the Ottoman Royal Court. These silk textiles, serving as economic and diplomatic commodities for the Ottoman treasury, had been

1 Inalcik (2008: 14).
2 Inalcik (2008: 221).
3 Inalcik (2008: 221).
4 Atasoy, Denny, Mackie & Tezcan (2001: 165).

exported to Europe, especially to Poland (Lechia) and Russia. Valuable textiles ordered by the kings, princes, nobles and churches of Eastern Europe, had been carried quite safely by royal Armenian, Jewish, Tatar and Persian merchants through Istanbul, Bulgaria, Dobruja, Moldova and by the Prut River to their final destination in Krakow, Poland. Silk was a great source of income for the Ottoman treasury, starting from the entry of the raw silk to the Ottoman territory, through the weaving process until its export as a processed commodity. "From the beginning of the 16th century, Poland had been the most reputable European client of silk textiles from Bursa. Privileges granted to the Polish kings by Sultan Suleiman the Magnificent for their orders of silk textiles had been re-granted in time; with every new agreement providing Polish kings and Polish people with the necessary fabrics from Turkey. Particularly assigned men were being sent to buy huge amounts of silk textiles from Turkey. In order to get tax exemption for the textiles bought for the Polish king, ambassadors had to ask permission from the Turkish head of state".[5] "From Moldova to Principality of Moscow, to Poland, the rulers of Eastern Europe were appointing their merchants to buy Bursa textiles. For example, in 1567, the Polish king granted tax exemption to a merchant to buy silk Bursa textiles worth 4000 gold ducats".[6]

Political relations between Ottoman Empire and Poland (Lechia) had begun in 1414 with the two ambassadors sent by Polish King Wladyslaw Jagiello to the palace of Mehmet Çelebi I in Bursa. Relations between the Ottoman Empire and Lechia had a history of over 600 years, filled with commerce, interactions of art and culture, changing political balances, conflicts, wars, defeats and victories. Bilateral relations improved from 15th through 18th centuries. "In this era in which the interactive trade becomes so important, the two capitals Bursa and Krakow stand prominent. Vivid art ambiance in both capital cities induce goods of trade. Textiles are the most important commodity among the two countries. Luxury fabrics produced in Bursa are exported to Poland and used to dress the nobility and in religious ritual clothes, and beyond their value of use, carpets and other textiles are regarded as the most prestigious decorative goods in royal courts and churches".[7] "In historical Krakow textile customs documents between 1589–1640 there are numerous records of silk satin, damask, velvet and other fabrics of Turkish silk, imported as rolls or pieces as well as covers and waistbands from Ottoman Empire".[8] "In one record of 1603, a merchant was reported to import 495 arshins of velvet, 395 arshins of silk (kitajka)".[9]

---

[5] Dalsar (1960: 156–157).
[6] Inalcik (2008: 14).
[7] Ölçer (2014: 10).
[8] Atasoy, Uluç (2012: 69).
[9] Atasoy, Uluç (2012: 69).

Ill. 1. Saint Mary, unknown artist, mid-15th century (National Museum, Warsaw). Right: Detail from her dress

Ottoman textiles were also featured in religious paintings. In the central piece of a triptych dated 1460, now in the inventory of Warsaw National Museum, shows Saint Mary, St. Philippe and St. James, in which Saint Mary is depicted in a velvet dress with a design composed of three dots (*çintemani*) and crescents. In traditional Turkish arts, *çintemani* is used as a talisman for protection against evil eye. It is one of the favourite motives in Ottoman tile art, in kaftans of sultans and in Uşak carpets.

The Christian figures depicted in the paintings of Orthodox churches and on a variety of garments for priests, ritual robes and altar clothes, are adorned on special fabrics with gold threads. "For example, when an inventory carried out in Wawel Catedral in Krakow in 1562, a great number of Ottoman silks, including a sleeveless priest gown made of Turkish *kemha (casula ex rubea kamkha Turchica)* had been documented".[10]

The valuable *kemhas* and *seraser* fabrics weaved with gold and silver threads, adorned with Christian symbols bear typical technical and figurative characteristics of Ottoman textiles and art. In order to show the grandeur of the Polish Church, the Bursa textiles woven with gold and silk had been used in clergy dresses.

10 Atasoy, Uluç (2012: 69).

A red *kemha* ritual robe, dated to 1606 and exhibited in Krakow Lateran Monastery, features an extensive number of carnation motives, which were common in products of Bursa weavers in the second half of the 16th century. Saint Mary, figures of saints and the seal of the founder of the monastery were adorned in the roundels placed in the wide bands at the front and back of the robe, in order to give the robe its religious purpose.

Ill. 2. *Kemha* ritual robe, dated 1606 (Krakow Lateran Monastery)

The adorned textiles in the collections of churches consist of either textiles that were purchased from Bursa, or the special political gifts from the Istanbul Orthodox Patriarchate to churches of Poland and to Polish royal courts, aiming to establish guardianship. "For example in 1548, a 'damask fabric with cross figures' was ordered from an Ottoman merchant named 'Musheddin'. In the custom records of Krakow, the city's life of trade during the end of 16th century till the middle of 17th century can be seen, including the details of textile and clothing export: Turkish garments, velvets with coloured, black and red patterns or brown textiles blended with velvet, lower quality black or coloured silk fabrics, silkalines of Turkish or Tatar origin, a vast amount of blue, green or red, good quality or bad imitations of Chines silk fabrics, Turkish woollen fabrics or silks of *grubrin* kind, fabrics in arshins or rolls. Damascus made *seraser* silk fabrics and velvets and silk satins weaved with gold threads were accepted as the most beautiful and most valuable among these exported fabrics".[11]

The custom records in Bursa and Krakow shows that the trade relations between these two cities were not only limited to the trade of textiles. The records show that three Polish merchants visited the *qadi* of Bursa to ask permission to buy raw silk and dyes; and Turkish weavers were sent to Poland in the 17th century.

The relations that had begun in the 15th century between Ottoman Empire and Poland were continued by sending of ambassadors throughout the 17th and

[11] Biedrońska-Słota (2014: 87).

18th centuries, with wars, peaces, political, commercial and cultural exchanges. The records show that at different times, a total of 150 Polish ambassadors of a variety of ranks were sent to Ottoman Empire. "The board of ambassadors would often bring clothings as gifts. In the departure ceremony of King Zygmunt August's ambassador in 1557, (...) the ambassador was gifted with an innerwear weaved with gold threads, a full outer wear, again weaved with gold thread, and several *kemha* shirts".[12]

The life of the court in Istanbul, reception ceremonies, the traditions of the local people and religious ceremonies, as noted in the reports of ambassadors, had created admiration in Poland, and affected the lifestyle. Eastern style interior designs decorated with valuable carpets, Ottoman women's and men's wear styles were in vogue. By the coronation of Stephan Batory – prince of Transylvania (Ardel), an autonomous principality connected to Ottoman Empire – as the king of Poland, the Ottoman influence on Poland's fashion interpreted by Hungarian nobility, peaked in Poland. Following the easternization of art and fashion preferences, the nobility of Poland adopted the Turkish, Iranian and Hungarian style with luxury silk textiles, velvets, *seraser* kaftans, shirts and belts as their own national style. Noblemen and representatives of states of military or civilian rank posed for self-portraits in kaftans made of Bursa textiles such as brocard, *seraser* and velvet. Headdresses with plumes were loved and used by both nobility and ordinary people.

In the portrait of Jan Krysztof Tarnowski, painted at the end of the 17th century and exhibited today in the Warsaw National Museum, with the details of inner and outer pieces worn, the belt around his waist and plumed headdress, his coat of arms with crescent and star reflects the eastern style in fashion.

In the portrait of Janusz Radziwill, dated to 1652 and exhibited today in Krakow, Royal Wawel Castle, he wears a red belt around the waist of his Ottoman style clothing, and is equipped with a mace or *şeşber* and a dagger in his headdress.

The mace or *şeşbers*, embellished with precious stones and used in ceremonies in Ottoman Empire, were adopted by the European nobility as a symbol of power. Polish noblemen posed for their portraits, carrying such weapons to emphasise their nobility and power.

In another example dated to before 1650, Polish noblemen Zbigniew Ossolinski poses for a portrait with his three sons. The blue kaftan, lined with fur, apart from the arms which narrow towards the wrists, bears great resemblance to Ottoman kaftans. Ossolinski wears an Ottoman style belt on top of his inner garment buttoned in the front. The table in the background is draped with a Western Anatolian (Transylvania) carpet for decoration.

---

12 Biedrońska-Słota (2014: 87).

Ill. 3. Portrait of Jan Krysztof Tarnowski, late 17th century (National Museum, Warsaw)

Ill. 4. Portrait of Janusz Radziwill, circa 1652 (Royal Wawel Castle, Krakow)

In the early 17th century Stanislaw Koniecpolski brought Armenian, Jewish and Turkish craftsmen to Poland and founded workshops for weaving Ottoman style fabrics. When the supply capacity of the textile workers in Bursa fell short to meet the increasing demand from Polish nobility for Ottoman or Iranian style belts, new ateliers were established in Istanbul in the 18th century, by Armenian masters Ewon Mikonowicz and Yakup Petrowicz. These ateliers, in time, moved closer to the borders towards Poland, to get closer to the clients.

Ill. 5. Portrait of Zbigniew Ossolinski before 1650 (Royal Castle, Warsaw)

Talented Ottoman masters trained local textile workers as master weavers, and in time, they produced belts similar in quality to Ottoman belts. Some of the belts were marked with "date in Roman numerals, and in some, such as possible Ottoman Armenian master Yakub Petrowicz's, the name of the weaver or the atelier was marked".[13]

Most of the Ottoman textiles mentioned in the archival documents, and kept in museums and collections in Poland are primarily acquired as diplomatic presents or through purchase. However in time, the number of Turkish properties in Polish possession increased tenfold through spoils of war. In 1683, Ottoman vizier Kara Mustafa Paşa besieged Vienna. This war resulted in the defeat of Ottomans, due to Polish king Jan Sobieski's support of the Habsburgs. After the war, in a letter to his wife, Sobieski narrates the victory with awe and admiration. In the letter, he pays particular attention to the royal tent of Kara Mustafa Paşa, which with its bath, garden and fountains resembled a real palace. Among the possessions of Jan Sobieski's "there are many Ottoman textiles listed; a large, red curtain with silver embroidery, a *seraser* kaftan, 23 shirts, four chairs covered in velvet, a seven weaving looms wide red bedpost curtain with green and gold flower patterns, and a flag with gold lettering on a very durable silk fabric called *ermezin*, possibly acquired during the Hotin War with the Ottomans in 1621".[14]

The largest collection of remaining tents from the 100.000 tents acquired from Ottomans after the Siege of Vienna resides in the Wavel Royal Castle today. "These were mostly donated by the heirs of those who fought in the Siege of Vienna".[15]

For 600 years, through war and peace, the Ottoman language, traditions, fashion and esthetic preferences had been an influence in Poland. Although they do not

13 Atasoy, Uluç (2012: 69).
14 Atasoy, Uluç (2012: 179).
15 Atasoy (2000: 242).

share a common border, the Ottoman Empire and Poland, Bursa and Krakow, created a common history based on culture and art, leaving an imprint on the present, through the Silk Road and thanks to the glamorous sheen of silk.

BIBLIOGRAPHY

Atasoy (2000) = Nurhan Atasoy; *Otağ-ı Hümayun Osmanlı Çadırları* (The Royal Tent Ottoman tents). Istanbul: Aygaz, 2000.

Atasoy, Denny, Mackie & Tezcan (2001) = Nurhan Atasoy; Walter B. Denny; Luise W. Mackıe; Hülya Tezcan, *İpek; Osmanlı Dokuma Sanatı* (Silk; Ottoman Art of Weaving). London: Azimuth Editions, 2001.

Atasoy, Uluç (2012) = Nurhan Atasoy; Lale Uluç. *Osmanlı Kültürünün Avrupa'daki Yansımaları: 1453–1699* (Reflections of Ottoman Culture in Europe: 1453–1699). Istanbul: Armaggan, Turkish Cultural Foundation, 2012.

Biedrońska-Słota (2014) = Beata Biedrońska-Słota, "Polonya'daki Türk Dokumaları – Polonya-Türkiye İlişkilerindeki İşlev ve Rolleri" (Turkish Weaves in Poland – Functions and Roles in Poland-Turkey Relations). In *Uzak Komşu Yakın Anılar Türkiye Polonya İlişkilerinin 600. Yılı* (Distant Neighbor Close Memories – 600th year of Turkey-Poland Relations.). Istanbul: Sabancı University Sabancı Museum 2014.

Dalsar (1960) = Fahri Dalsar, *Türk Sanayi ve Ticaret Tarihinde Bursa'da İpekçilik* (Silk Industry in Bursa within the History of Turkish Industry and Trade). Istanbul University Publication. Istanbul: 1960.

Inalcık (2008) = Halil INALCIK, *Türkiye Tekstil Tarihi Üzerine Araştırmalar* (Studies on Textile History of Turkey). Istanbul: İş Bankası Kültür Yayınları, 2008.

Ölçer (2014) = Nazan ÖLÇER, "Önsöz" [Preface] *Uzak Komşu Yakın Anılar, Türkiye Polonya İlişkilerinin 600. Yılı* (Distant Neighbor Close Memories – 600th year of Turkey-Poland Relations). Istanbul: Sabancı University Sabancı Museum, 2014.

PART FOUR: TECHNIQUE AND TRADITION THROUGHOUT ASIA

Natalia Shabalina
South-Ural State University, National Research University

Colour is a sign of national traditional ornamental art

In this article author considers colour as a sign of national traditional ornamental art in the material culture of the Turkic folk art and the Slavic peoples, inhabiting the territory of the Southern Urals. The author determined the dependence of colour from natural-climatic, socio-economic factors, certain religious and philosophical foundations of the nation. The principle of integrated compositional and colouristic organisation of artistic decoration in the home and the national costume formed on the basis of these factors.

Key words: problem of colour; tradition; national art; ornament.

The colour in the traditional artistic culture of the Turkic peoples

The issue of colour in art criticism has different aspects of study – semantic-semiotic, figuratively, emotional, structural and compositional, stylistic, traditional and national. Colour choice has great importance in determining the national colours and the identity of an object or set of items and, in general, the whole culture of the traditional ethnic life. The content-structural complex of traditional folk decoration of dwellings and the national costume concentrates in the colour ensemble. The national-ethnic basis of colour is interdependent on other issues: ideological (religious, cosmogonic), gender, natural-climatic, socio-economic. These issues point to the priorities of human economic activity.

While discussing the issue of colour as a sign of national traditional ornamental art, we explore the folk art culture of Turkic and Slavic people dwelling on the territory of the Urals. The study of Bashkir national art leads many researchers to the analysis and characterisation of nomadic dwellings – tents and, its successor, the house the objects that furnish it.[1] The process of establishing the settlements of Bashkir preceded seasonal wandering in the spring and summer followed by setting up camp in the autumn and winter. The permanent settlements belonged to the period of entry into the Russian Bashkir State. During this era, there were villages that became population centres and regional departments. The process of active formation of villages in the southern steppe regions of the Bashkir settlement started at the beginning of the 19th century.

A wooden frame was the constructive basis of the yurt. A smooth, warm white felt covered it on the outside and inside. The whiteness of the felt symbolised savagery and moral purity. Goods made of felt were often ornamented in engineering applications, or by racking coloured wool felt mat in the background. Ornamented felts shingled the tents and expressed views of the Kosmogonichenskie Bashkir. The yurt is one of the most stable features in the Bashkir concept of the harmony of world order. The shape of the yurt was round, which they believed symbolised harmony.

The organisation of the interior corresponded to the constructive and meaningful form of the yurt. Traditionally, the centre of the yurt had a low soft focus. A chest was placed in front of the tent on a carved or painted base. In this chest, folded warm clothes, carpets, quilts, pillows were kept and bandaged with a special tape with a floral pattern. The textile design of the yurt was consistent with the lifestyle of the nomads, who in the course of migrations needed to carry their entire mobile home and all household items themselves. Woollen goods kept people warm and created comfort in the house.

The yurt along with its inhabitants is a holistic organism. So, we can see a colouristic unity between the interior and the national costume. The relationship of the constructive and decorative elements of the interior creates a united composition. This composition is determined by the role each family member. The Turkic master of ornamental art is enriched by a rich colour palette. One ornamental composition included red, yellow, blue, green, white and black colour, but kept the innate appeal of the composition. Bashkir masters used a background colour in the embroidery (ill. 1). The colour contrast characteristic of the general concept of the Bashkir home interior and the national costume drew from the protective power of vital energy, and a healthy lifestyle. However, a polyphony of colours can be found in the traditional art of other nationalities – in Turkic art this was due to the specific

---

[1] Aminev (2005); Akhmerov (1996); The peoples of Bashkortostan (2002); Rudenko (1925); Shitova (1984); Yanbukhtina (2006).

Ill. 1. Ritual towel, beginning of 20th century, hand weaving

Ill. 2. Counting Russian embroidery on the towel late 19th–early 20th century, the southern Urals

climatic conditions of Bashkir settlement (the steppes), and their economic activities regarding animal husbandry. An explanation for the predominance of the colour in the Turkic art can be found in the natural needs of this ethnic group to make a rich palette of colours in clothing and household furnishings of the home. Some noticeable feature of the various geometric and plant ornamental forms are the dotted, mosaic, often asymmetrical rhythms of composite structural formations. For example, the use of decoration pieces of graded diamonds, 8-petal rosette that are so universal in art shaped the expressive language of every national culture through various techniques of unity or contrast of colours, smooth or discontinuous general configurations of geometric shapes or stylised images (ill. 3).

Ill. 3. Palace Bashkir middle of the 20th century, hand weaving, Chelyabinsk Regional Museum

Ill. 4. Fragment of the shaft of the Bashkir shoes with a "kuskar" pattern

Home for the Bashkir has always been the embodiment of the materialised understanding of world order. The traditional nomadic lifestyle and had a very strong influence on the interior of the home along with the tradition of building wooden huts or mud-brick houses. The researchers classified the complex textile items decorating the Bashkir home in terms of the material and manufacturing equipment.[2] The ornamental compositions often contain stylised ram horns. Many researchers think this tradition was borrowed from the people of Siberia.[3] In the ancient Turkic world, the "space bar" was the most common. It brings good luck, wealth and progeny. The characteristic spiral S-shaped motifs of Turkic ornament were constantly encountered in the design of various household textile goods and elements of costume (for example, felt and cloth shoes). Craftsmen used the multicoloured kuskarny pattern in different techniques (appliqué, tambour embroidery) (ill. 4).

The oriental ornament "islimi" was often used in tambour embroidery technique. "Running stalk" was the main islimi motif. It embodied the idea of constantly evolving and renewing life. Traditional tambour late 19th–early 20th century Bashkir embroidery subtly varied the stylised fast and free "floral" pattern, to included lined, asymmetrical compositions (ills. 5, 6). The expressive possibilities of colour embroidery gave a poetic richness to the colourful decorative woven fabric goods and brought joy to the home. Woven fabrics with geometric patterns, usually made with the technique of counting stitches (strochevaya embroidery, countable smooth, slanting stitch, Perevicolour). Weaving strictly focused on the threads in the cloth used. That is why it was an organic compound pattern with accentuated geometric properties.

The absence of zoomorphic and anthropomorphic motifs was a feature of Bashkir embroideries. This depended on the principles of the Islamic religion. On the other hand, geometric patterns, in which the red colour predominated, were similar to traditional Russian designs (ill. 2). Wall and floor rugs, tablecloths, towels and large curtains were an extensive part of the homespun items of decor in nomadic and

---

[2] Shitova (2006); Yanbukhtina (1993: 30).

[3] Shitova (2006: 195).

Ill. 5. Bashkir woman's apron, the beginning of the 20th century, the southern Urals, crochet, Chelyabinsk Regional Museum

Ill. 6. Bashkir woman's dress, the beginning of the 20th century, the southern Urals, crochet, Chelyabinsk Regional Museum

stationary housing. Large homespun items had an important place in the decoration of the living space. Woven products could structurally separate the interior (the curtain – "sharshau") into two halves or united space. The female half was bright and the second male half was terse. The bright, rich decoration of the yurt was determined by the semi-nomadic way of life. The monotone painted landscapes of the steppes were transformed by Turkic masters into bright colours in their products. As a result, the principle of ensemble in the compositional integrity of the home and the national costume was formed under the influence of climatic, socio-economic factors and religious backgrounds. Each structure and element of the ensemble created unity and harmony of living space.

Ill. 7. Russian Sarafan, the end of 19th–20th centuries (Chelyabinsk Regional Museum)

COLOUR IN THE TRADITIONAL ARTISTIC CULTURE OF THE SLAVIC PEOPLES

The house and home of the Slavic worldview was a symbol of the universe. Soviet scientists researching the history of the ancient Slavs came to the conclusion that paganism was the basis of the material and spiritual aspects of the life of the Slavs.[4] Paganism had always existed alongside Christianity throughout the history of Russia. The home was a kind of reference point in space and time.[5] The folk traditions and worldview of the peasants determined how the order of things would be divided. The solar symbols decorating the doors and windows at home and the woven items of interior decoration were also explained by their protective functions (ill. 7, 8).

A timbered granary square shape was a model for planning all types of Russian peasant dwellings. A diagonal model with the stove located in one corner of the house was the most common internal layout. The space was divided into a male and female half. The women's place was the baking corner and the area leading from it to the opposite wall. This space was equipped with a variety of items for crafts. In winter a loom was installed. The location of all the objects and elements in the house depended on the position of the oven.

The "Red (front) corner" was located diagonally across from the oven. The "Shrine" was the main accent. All the important family events were celebrated in this part of the house. The icon in the "red corner" was an important attribute of a Russian dwelling. The icon was decorated and ornamented with an embroidered towel. The composition and colour of the towel gave information about the ethnic group of the peasants who lived in the house.

---

4 Baiburin (1983), Russian (1967), Rybakov (1981), Tsivyan (1978).
5 Nekrasova (1988: 43).

The house gave a representation of the peasants and the outside world and represented the boundary between them. Isolation and demarcation in the macrocosm and the creation of a safe space in the microcosm was one of the important functions of the home.[6] However, contact with the outside world were a necessary condition of human life. Therefore, the house should include an entrance.

On one side of the wall, windows and doors separated man from the outside world while, on the other hand, giving an opportunity to connect with the outside world. The symbols decorating the doors and windows explained the need to make the boundary permeable. Russian peasants thought that windows should be protected against the penetration of the foreign, harmful and impure. Windows were decorated with a carved window frame on the outside and inside by curtains, which were richly ornamented according to the Russian peasants' concept of protective talismans. Floral designs and geometric shapes stylised admitted the zoomorphic and anthropomorphic motifs used in the patterns and expressed their protective function. They were a symbol of the well-being and happiness of the peasants living in the house. The diamond shape, sometimes square, placed at an angle was the most common form of ornamental design for the Russian peasants. Diamonds were the main motif of ornamental compositions and were combined in various ways: intersected into one another, bonded chain overlap angles, arranged in staggered rows, etc. Sometimes the diamond was replaced by a circle or rosettes (ill. 2). Russian researchers (G. S. Maslova, B. V. Rybakov) attributed these forms with the idea of the sun. Sunshine is a cult of worship as can be observed in solar technology.[7]

The interior of the house was designed in a circular rhythm. For example, vertically striped curtains overlapped the horizontal canopy. The solar image with its semantic meaning was created by a circle and semicircle. On the other hand, the semicircle can be associated with the protection of peasant dwellings. The door, entry, threshold and porch were of a high semiotic significance. Ornamental towels, which were protective in nature, hung over the door.

The decoration of the floor with carpets had a special importance for peasants. In the Trans-Uralian villages carpets were called "trails".[8] Colourful woven carpet "trails" were spread out along the wooden floorboards in the direction of the entrance as a symbol of easy entry and exit, easy goodbye wishes or invitations into the house. Trans-Ural masters wove woollen floor carpet "trails" with the addition of flax yarn.

[6] Tsivyan (1978).
[7] Maslova (1978), Rybakov (1981).
[8] Shabalina (2007: 93).

Ill. 8. Shadrinsk "footpath", the middle of the 20th century, wool, hand weaving

Rhythmically alternating coloured bands created the composition and unified image of the carpet. Broad horizontal colourful bands separated the intermediate narrow strips ("podzorinki") that divided one colour from another. South Ural masters preferred to use bright colours of yarn (from the beginning of the 20th century natural dyes were replaced by chemical aniline). Craftsmen alternated the colour saturation from dense to light (ill. 8). Many weavers said that colour was important in weaving. Bright colour was associated with sunlight – the universal solar symbolism used in the ornament carpets "trails". This involved a diamond image as in the Bashkir carpet, but with a common configuration and concise single colour scheme. The design consisted of a diamond, different in size, inscribed into each other, located in the centre, lined or continuous rows of colour intermingled, forming a carpet. The magnitude and angle of the diamonds was constantly varied. The rhythm geometric composition (a broken line running diagonally, or straight – horizontally) was determined by the colour. The floor was covered by woven carpets (sometimes overlapping each other). Colourful carpets filled the house with bright light and warmth (ill. 9). Often the carpets were located continuously in two adjacent rooms by laying them over the threshold of the home's interior doors "in torsion". Thus, the peasants expressed the integrity of the interior of the hut.

In the ensemble of the Trans-Ural home, the wall carpet fits harmoniously.[9] In general, the internal living space was filled with light from the bright sun of the pattern of various composite woven fabrics. On the territory of the Middle Urals, woven decor replaced wall-painting. Tufted carpets with floral patterns were prevalent in this area. For example, the village of Lower Sinyachikha is now a museum of wooden architecture.[10] The ornamentation of the ceiling and walls of the huts

9 Shabalina (2003).
10 Catalogue (1988).

Ill. 9.
Wall carpet, village Canash, Urals, the middle of the 20th century, wool, hand weaving

along with the colourful painting on the wood created the integrity of the interior peasant dwellings. The decor could create a harmoniously integrated ensemble in the Russian peasant dwellings. The uniform composition and colour organisation of the subject-spatial environment was the base for specific ethnic traditions (ill. 10). Colour has a cultural and social significance. Woven products, as well as many other attributes of human life, were divided into everyday-casual, holiday and funeral. The semantic preference and meaning of the substantive content and structure of the home and national costume changed over time. Traditional peasant life changed over time.

Each ethnic group in the multiethnic structure of the population of the Urals had their own principles regarding the organisation of housing and clothing. These rules were based on their unique worldview, experience and tradition and this in turn informed their own knowledge. The colouristic organisation, subordination and correlation of all goods

Ills. 10–11. Fragments of wall paintings, the village of Lower Sinyachikha, the middle Urals, the end of the 19th century

and elements with each other and with people, society and nature were the main characteristic of the interior of the national housing and the national costume. As a result, ethnic groups formed a united national image of traditional ornamental art.

Bibliography

Aminev 2005 = Z. Aminev, Cosmogonic beliefs of the ancient Bashkir. Ufa 2005, p. 140. (Аминев З. Г. Космогонические воззрения древних башкир. Уфа, 2005. 140 с.).

Akhmerov 1996 = R. Akhmerov, On the origins of decorative arts of the Bashkir people. Ufa 1996. (Ахмеров Р. Б. Об истоках декоративно-прикладного искусства башкирского народа. Уфа, 1996).

Baiburin 1983 = A. Baiburin, Real Estate in the rites and beliefs of Eastern Slavs. Moscow, 1983. (Байбурин А. К. Жилище в обрядах и представлениях восточных славян. Москва, 1983).

Catalogue 1988 = Catalogue Ural folk paintings of peasant houses and household items in the collection Lower Sinyachikha Museum. Collection I. D. Samoilova/ Samoilov I. D. Sverdlovsk, 1988, p. 199. (Каталог уральской народной росписи крестьянских домов и предметов быта в собрании Нижнесинячихинского музея-заповедника: Коллекция И. Д. Самойлова/ И. Д. Самойлов И.Д. Свердловск, 1988. 199 с.).

Maslova 1978 = G. Maslova Ornament Russian folk embroidery as a historical source. Moscow, 1978, p.174. (Маслова Г. С. Орнамент русской народной вышивки как исторический источник. Москва, 1978).

The peoples of Bashkortostan 2002 = The peoples of Bashkortostan: historical and ethnographic essays. Ufa, 2002, p. 504.: Table., Maps. (Народы Башкортостана: историко--этнографические очерки. 2-еизд., доп. Уфа, 2002. 504 с.: табл., рис., ил., карты).

Nekrasova 1988 = M. Nekrasova, Ensemble as image system// Art Ensemble. Art object, interior, architecture, environment/ status, and scientific. Ed. M.

Nekrasova. M., 1988, p. 43–96. (Некрасова М. А. Ансамбль как образная система// Искусство ансамбля. Художественный предмет, интерьер, архитектура, среда/ сост. и науч. ред. М. А. Некрасова. Москва, 1988. С. 43–96).

Rudenko 1925 = S. Rudenko, Bashkirs: Experience ethnological monographs. Part 2. Gen. Bashkir. Leningrad, 1925, p. 330. (Руденко С. И. Башкиры: Опыт этнологической монографии. Часть 2. Быт башкир. Ленинград, 1925. 330 с., ил.).

Russian 1967 = Russian. Historical and Ethnographic atlas. Agriculture. Peasant housing. Peasant Clothing (mid 19th – early 20th century)./ Ed. V. A. Alexandrov. Institute of Ethnography, USSR Academy of Sciences. Moscow, 1967. (Русские. Историко-этнографический атлас. Земледелие. Крестьянское жилище. Крестьянская одежда (середина XIX – начало XX в.) / под ред. В. А. Александрова. Ин-т этнографии АН СССР. Москва, 1967).

Rybakov 1981 = B. Rybakov, Ancient Slavicpaganism. Moscow, 1981, p. 608. (Рыбаков Б. А. Язычество древних славян. Москва, 1981. 608 с.).

Tsivyan 1978 = T. Tsivyan, archetypal image of the house in the popular mind// Proceedings of sign systems. T. 10. Tartu, 1978 (Цивьян Т. В. Архетипический образ дома в народном сознании// Труды по знаковым системам. Т. 10. Тарту, 1978).

Shabalina 2003 = N. Shabalina, "Kanashinskie path" (of Trans-Ural carpet weaving): From the track pad// Arts and Crafts. Moscow, 2003, no. 3, p. 15. (Шабалина Н. М.

«Канашинские тропинки» (о зауральском ковроткачестве): Из путевого блокнота// Народное творчество. Москва, 2003 № 3. С. 15).

Shabalina 2007 = N. Shabalina, Traditional crafts and trades of the Southern Urals (late 19th - mid 20th century). Chelyabinsk, SouthUralprofessionalinstitute, 2007, p. 148. (Шабалина Н. М. Традиционные художественные ремёсла и промыслы Южного Урала (вторая половина XIX – середина XX веков). Челябинск, Южно-Уральский профессиональный институт, 2007. 148 с.: ил.).

Shitova 1984 = S. Shitova, TraditionalsettlementsanddwellingsBashkir. Moscow, 1984 (Шитова, С. Н. Традиционные поселения и жилища башкир. Москва, 1984).

Shitova 2006 = S. Shitova, Folk Art: felts, carpets and fabrics in the southern Bashkir/ S. N. Shitova. Ufa, 2006, p. 200. (Шитова С. Н. Народное искусство: войлоки, ковры и ткани у южных башкир/ С. Н. Шитова. Уфа, 2006. 200 с: ил.).

Yanbukhtina 1993 = A. Yanbukhtina, Traditions in the decoration of the Bashkir home. Ufa, 1993 (Янбухтина А. Г. Народные традиции в убранстве башкирского дома. Уфа, 1993).

Yanbukhtina 2006 = A. Yanbukhtina, Decorative art of Bashkortostan. 20th Century: From tamgi to avant-garde. Ufa, 2006, p. 224. (Янбухтина А. Г. Декоративное искусство Башкортостана. XX век: От тамги до авангарда. Уфа, 2006. 224 с: ил.).

Racep Karadag
Marmara University

Yusuf Yildiz
Complete Analysis Laboratories, Inc. Analytical Chemistry Department, New Jersey

Characterisation of dyes, metal threads and silk yarns from 16–18th-centuries Ottoman silk brocades

Abstract

The technique and dyeing properties regarding Ottoman silk brocade were very important for the Far East and Europe in the 16th–18th centuries. Therefore, in this study, the analysis of dyestuff, metal thread and silk yarn samples present in some 16th–18th-centuries Ottoman silk textile samples were performed according to non-destructive and micro analysis methods. Silk yarns with yellow, blue, orange, brown, red, and green colours were selected for the analysis from Topkapi Place Museum in Istanbul. Some analytical methods were used for the identification of dyestuffs, yarn, metal threads and weaving techniques in different Ottoman silk brocades.

One of the most useful procedures is for the determination of metal threads. This is a simple method that provides information on the chemical composition of sample surfaces and the chemical analysis of metal threads. Dye source, yarn characterisation, weaving techniques and metal threads were identified in the 16th–18th centuries Ottoman Silk Brocades.

Introduction

Ottoman silk textiles reached their zenith in the 16th century. The wide use of silk textiles in furniture, home textiles and clothing displayed the wealth of the Ottoman court. Silk textiles used for clothing were made out of silk, silver and gold threads. Kaftans were crafted either with gold threads, silver threads or with both gold and silver threads.

While Ottoman textiles were produced in multiple locations, Istanbul and Bursa were the only centres to supply the Topkapi Palace (Ottoman court). Textiles produced for the palace were subjected to strict quality controls. While numerous museums around the world hold Ottoman textiles in their collections, the Topkapi Palace Museum has the largest and most comprehensive collection in the world. These textiles often represent the highest form of cultural, artistic and socio-economic discoveries of their eras. Information embedded in these textiles, therefore, is not only important to Turkey's textile sector, but is of utmost value for the world's textile heritage.

Ottoman silk brocades were investigated by non-destructive and microanalysis methods in the Topkapi Palace Museum as well as others. Multi analytical techniques were used for the analyses by TCF Cultural Heritage Preservation and Natural Dyes Laboratory.

Analyses are very important for the restoration and conservation of historical textiles. Samples are analysed according to non-destructive and microanalysis methods. The most widely used methods are HPLC-PDA (high performance liquid chromatography with diode array detection), SEM-EDX (scanning electron microscopy with energy dispersive X-ray), colour measurements and technical analysis. The identification of dyes is one of the most important aims in the scientific examination of paintings, textiles, illuminated manuscripts and other historic and archaeological materials. Thus, several analytical techniques were used – for example thin layer chromatography, high performance liquid chromatography[1] gas chromatography/mass spectrometry, UV-visible spectrometry[2] reversed phase liquid chromatography and capillary electrophoresis with electrospray mass spectrometric detection, FTIR spectroscopy and Raman spectroscopy.[3] Of these techniques, high performance liquid chromatography (HPLC) using a diode-array detection (DAD) is ideally suit-

1 Surowiec et al. (2003); Clementi et al. (2006); Degano et al. (2009); Erkan (2011); Bechtold et al. (2003); Bechtold, Mahmud-Ali, Mussak (2007); Bechtold, Mahmud-Ali et al. (2007); Vankar, Shanker, Verma (2007); Vankar et al. (2008); Das, Maulik, Bhattacharya (2008); Zarkogianni (2011); Surowiec, Nowik, Trojanowicz (2008).

2 Deveoglu, Torgan, Karadag (2012).

3 Baliarsingh et al. (2012).

Ill. 1.
Kaftan, inv. no. 13/529,
Topkapi Place Museum
(Photo: R. Karadag)

ed to the identification of dye samples from museum collections especially.[4] The CIEL*a*b* (1976)-system was introduced to describe colour as a result of these three factors. This system is a three-dimensional space, with coordinate axes L*, a* and b*. L* denotes the brightness of the colour (L*=0: black, L*=100: white); a* represents the green-red axis (a* negative: green, a* positive: red) and b* represents the blue-yellow axis (b* negative: blue, b* positive: yellow). Each colour can be represented as a set of values for L*, a* and b*, and consequently as a point in this colour space.[5]

EXPERIMENTAL TECHNICAL ANALYSIS

An optical microscope is used for yarn or fibre characterisation of historical textiles. In this study the historical samples were investigated using an OLYMPUS SZ61 (SZ2-ILST, camera C18U). In this work some historical textile art objects were analysed. One of them is inventory number is 13/ 529 (ill. 1). The result is shown in Table 1 and Illustration 2.

---

[4] Meyer, Heinonen, Frankel (1998); Deveoglu (2012).
[5] Deveoglu, Sahinbaskan, et al. (2012).

Ill. 2.
Technique analysis image, inv. no. 13/529 (Topkapi Place Museum)

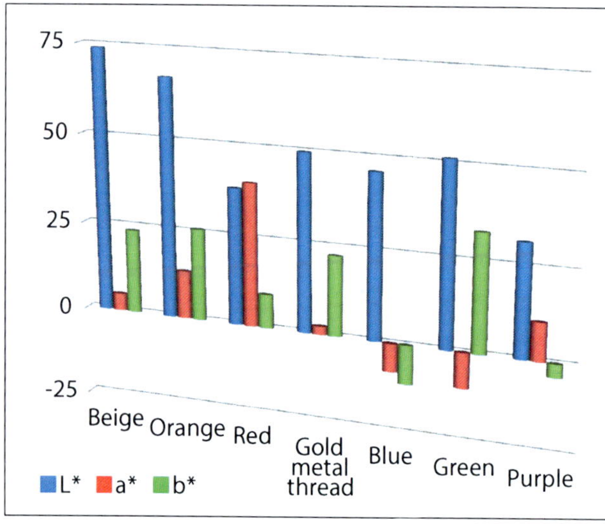

Ill. 3.
Colour value of inventory number 13/529

Extraction Procedure for HPLC Analysis of Historical Textiles

The extraction of historical textile samples were performed with a solution mixture of %37 HCl: MeOH: H_2O; 2:1:1; v: v:v) for 8 minutes at 100°C in small open tubes to extract the dyestuffs. After cooling under running cold tap water, the solution was evaporated to the point of solidification in a water bath at 65°C under a gently stream of nitrogen. The dry residue was dissolved in 200 µl of the mixture of MeOH: H_2O (2:1; v: v) or 200 µl DMF and was centrifuged at 4000 rpm for 10 min. 50 to 100 µl supernatant was injected into the HPLC apparatus.

Colour Measurements of Historical Textiles

L^*, a^* and b^* values for historical textiles and reproduced silk brocades were measured with a Konica Minolta CM-2300d Software Spectra Magic NX (6500 K, 45°). The colour value is shown Figure 3.

SEM-EDX Analysis

The characterisation of metal threads on historical textiles is important for the preservation of valuable cultural heritage. In this work the samples were investigated using a TESCAN VEGA3 Easy Probe Scanning Electron Microscope (SEM) equipped with energy dispersion spectroscopy (EDX with detector Bruker 410-M, software: Esprit 1.9). During this procedure, some metal fibres collected from historical textile materials were characterised.

Results

Optical microscope analysis results:

- The twisting direction of the yarns and metal threads was determined.
- Number of warp, inner warp, and weft inner yarns per centimetre in the historical textiles. The technique analysis results are shown Table 1.

Colour value analysis results:
The colour value analysis sheds light on the types of colours used in the original materials. The test results help guide colour selection for restoration purposes. Similarly, the colour values can help determine the colours to be used for fabric reproduction. This allows new fabrics to match the originals in colour.

Dye analysis results:

- The biological resources of the colouring compounds are identified in historical textiles. The result of 13/529 inventory number is shown in Table 2.
- The chemical and physical properties of the dyes are identified.
- Accurate dating of textiles can be enabled.
- The geographical region of historical textiles and their areas of production are identified.
- Proper restoration methods are identified based on the chemical and physical properties of the dyes found in the historical textiles.

- The same biological resources and colouring compounds can be used for re-productions.

Metal analysis results:

- The ratio of gold or silver in the metal threads is identified; 16th century textiles contain higher quantities of gold compared to textiles from the 18th century.
- Worthless metals (i.e. Cu, Zn, Cd) are identified in some 18th century textiles. Moreover, air pollutants (Cl, Mg, S, C) are identified in the threads.
- The metal threads are not alloys; all the metal threads are gilded.
- The thickness and width of the metal threads are identified. The metal threads are 5–7 micrometres thick and 140–180 micrometres wide in the 16th century, and 14–17 micrometres thick and 270–580 micrometres wide in the 18th century.
- The same metal (gold and silver) quantity can be used for re-productions.
- The same metal thickness and width can be used for re-productions.

The metal threads of some Ottoman brocade were analysed with the SEM-EDX in Topkapi Place Museum and their analysis results are shown in Table 3 along with the SEM images (ills. 4–6).

Conclusion

Our Laboratory (DATU) has served dozens of museums in Turkey and worldwide and has made significant contributions to the conservation and restoration of historical textiles.

Moreover, the know-how provided by DATU for the reproduction of Ottoman silk brocades has enabled the yarns of the new brocades to be dyed and weaved with the same materials, under similar conditions using the same techniques and dye sources. This has led to the identical reproduction of Ottoman silk brocades.

Reproduction of 16th Ottoman silk brocades proves to be extremely difficult, though not impossible.

DATU Analysis allows historical objects to be dated accurately and their geographical origins to be identified with greater precision.

Identifying the weaving structure, colour value, twist and spinning of yarns, chemical compositions of metal threads, dyestuffs and dye sources of art objects is made possible by DATU for the accurate and non-destructive restoration, conservation and cleaning methods of objects.

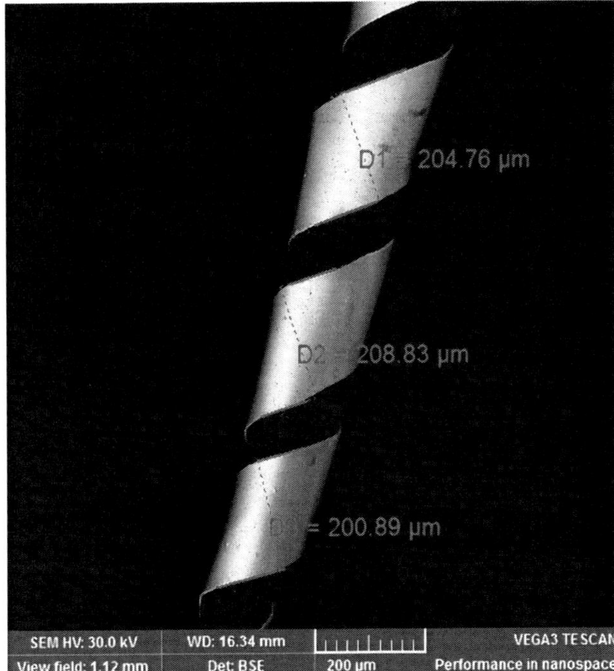

Ill. 4.
Metal thread SEM image, inv. no. 13/1830 (Topkapi Place Museum)

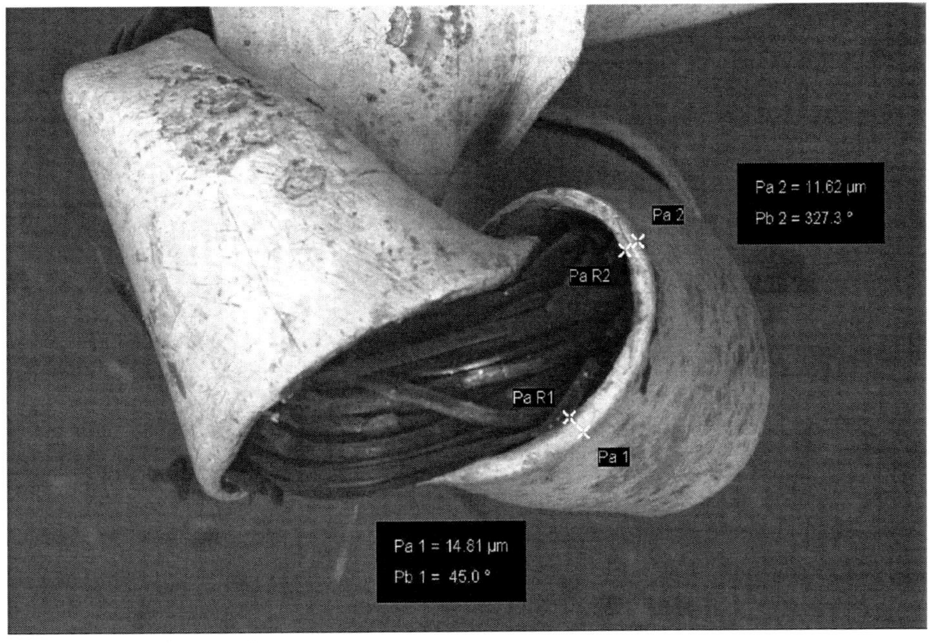

Ill. 4. Metal thread SEM image (Topkapi Place Museum)

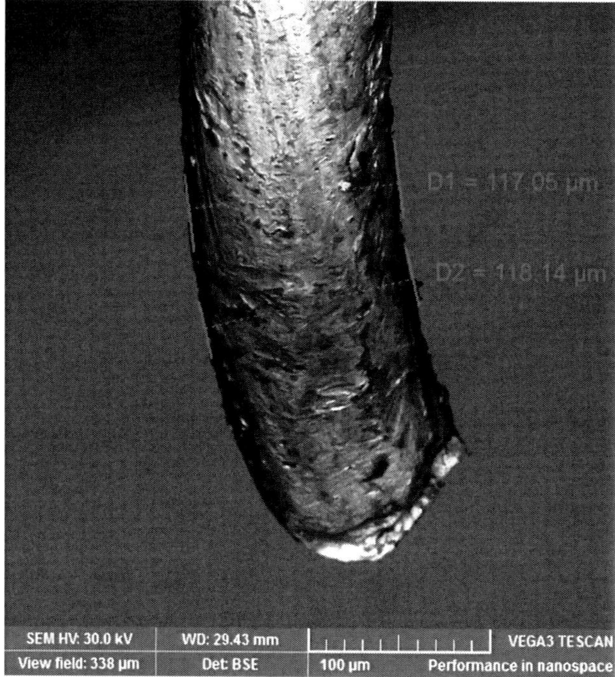

Ill. 6.
Metal thread SEM image
(Topkapi Place Museum)

Acknowledgements

Support from the Turkish Cultural Foundation and Armaggan company are gratefully acknowledged (www.turkishculturalfoundation.org; www.tcfdatu.org).

Bibliography

Surowiec et al. 2003 = Surowiec, I., Orska-Gawry, J., Biesaga, M., Trojanowicz, M., Hutta, M., Halko, R. and Urbaniak-Walczak, K., "Identification of natural dyestuff in archeological Coptic textiles by HPLC with fluorescence detection", *Anal. Lett.*, 2003, vol. 36, Issue 6, pp. 1211–1229.

Clementi et al. 2006 = Clementi, c., Miliani, c., Romani, A. and Favaro, G., "In situ fluorimetry: A powerful non-invasive diagnostic technique for natural dyes used in artefacts: Part I. Spectral characterization of orcein in solution, on silk and wool laboratory-standards and a fragment of Renaissance tapestry", *Spectrochim. Acta, Part A*, 2006, vol. 64, pp. 906–912.

Degano et al. 2009 = Degano, I., Ribechini, E., Modugno, F. and Colombini, M.P., "Analytical methods for the characterization of organic dyes in artworks and in historical textiles", *Appl. Spectrosc. Rev.*, 2009, vol. 44, Issue 5, pp. 363–410.

Erkan 2011 = Erkan, G., Sengul, K. and Kaya, S., J., "Dyeing of White and Indigo Dyed Cotton Fabrics with Mimosa Tenuiflora Extract", *Journal of Saudi Chemical Society*, 2011, vol. 18, Issue 2, pp. 139–148.

Bechtold et al. 2003 = Bechtold, T., Turcanu, A., Ganglberger, E. and Geissler, S., "Natural dyes in modern textile dyehouses – how to combine experiences of two centuries to meet the demands of the future", *J. Clean. Prod.*, 2003, vol. 11, Issue 5, pp. 499–509.

Bechtold, Mahmud-Ali, Mussak 2007 = Bechtold, T., Mahmud-Ali, A. and Mussak, R., "Natural dyes for textile dyeing: A comparison of methods to assess the quality of Canadian golden rod plant material", *Dyes and Pigments*, 2007, vol. 75, Issue 2, pp. 287–293.

Bechtold, Mahmud-Ali et al. 2007 = Bechtold, T., Mahmud-Ali, A. and Mussak, R.A.M., "Reuse of ash-tree (Fraxinus excelsior L.) bark as natural dyes for textile dyeing: process conditions and process stability", *Coloration Technology*, 2007, vol. 123, Issue 4, pp. 271–279.

Vankar, Shanker, Verma 2007 = Vankar, P.S., Shanker, R. and Verma, A., "Enzymatic natural dyeing of cotton and silk fabrics without metal mordants", *J. Clean. Prod.*, 2007, vol. 15, Issue 15, pp. 1441–1450.

Vankar et al. 2008 = Vankar, P.S., Shanker, R., Mahanta, D. and Tiwari, S.C., "Eco-friendly sonicator dyeing of cotton with Rubiacordifolia Linn. using biomordant", *Dyes and Pigments*, 2008, vol. 76, Issue 1, pp. 207–212.

Das, Maulik, Bhattacharya 2008 = Das, D., Maulik, S.R. and Bhattacharya, S.C., "Dyeing of wool and silk with Rheum emodi", *Indian J. Fiber Text. Res.*, 2008, vol. 33, Issue 2, pp. 163–170.

Zarkogianni 2011 = Zarkogianni, M., Mikropoulou, E., Varella, E. and Tsatsaroni, E., "Colour and fastness of natural dyes: revival of traditional dyeing techniques", *Colour. Technol.*, 2011, vol. 127, Issue 2, pp. 18–27.

Surowiec, Nowik, Trojanowicz 2008 = Surowiec, I., Nowik, W. and Trojanowicz, M., "Post-column deprotonation and complexation in HPLC as a tool for identification and structure elucidation of compounds from natural dyes of historical importance", *Microchim. Acta*, 2008, vol. 162, 393–404.

[13] Deveoglu, Torgan, Karadag 2012 = Deveoglu, O., Torgan, E. and Karadag, R., "The characterisation by liquid chromatography of lake pigments prepared from European buckthorn (Rhamnuscathartica L.) ", *J. Liq. Chrom. Relat. Technol.*, 2012, vol. 35, Issue 6, pp. 331–338.

Baliarsingh et al. 2012 = Baliarsingh, S., Panda, A.K., Jena, J., Das, T. and Das, N.B., "Exploring Sustainable Technique on Natural Dye Extraction from Native Plants for Textile: Identification of Colourants, Colourimetric Analysis of Dyed yarns and their Antimicrobial Evaluation", *J. Clean. Prod.*, 2012, vol. 37, pp. 257–264.

Meyer, Heinonen, Frankel 1998 = Meyer, A.S., Heinonen, M., and Frankel, E.N., "Antioxidant interactions of catechin, cyanidin, caffeic acid, quercetin, and ellagic acid on human LDL oxidant", *Food Chemistry*, 1998, vol. 61, Issue 1, pp. 71–75.

Deveoglu et al. 2012 = Deveoglu, O., Erkan, G., Torgan, E., and Karadag, R., "The evaluation of procedures for dyeing silk with buckthorn and walloon oak on the basis of colour changes and fastness characteristics", *Coloration Technologies*, 2012, vol. 129, Issue 3, pp. 223–231.

Deveoglu, Sahinbaskan, et al. 2012 = Deveoglu, O., Sahinbaskan, B.Y., Torgan, E., and Karadag, R., "Investigation on colour, fastness properties and HPLC-DAD analysis of silk fibres dyed with Rubiatinctorium L. and Quercusithaburensis Decaisne", *Coloration Technologies*, 2012, vol. 128, Issue 5, pp. 364–370.

Table 1. According to the technique analysis results.

16th century		18th century	
Spun		Spun	
spun warps	Z	spun warps	Z
spun wefts	Z	spun wefts	Z
number of warp yarns	120–125/cm	number of warp yarns	72- 98/cm or less
number of weft yarns	120–130/cm	number of weft yarns	72–98/cm or less
spun metal threads	S	spun metal threads	S
Quality	highest	quality	less

Table 2. Dyestuff analysis results of13/529 inventory number art object.

Inventory Number	Sample	Colour of Sample	Identified Dyestuff	Biological Source	Century
13/529	silk	salmon color	carminic acid Unidentified Rt: 25.685	*Dactylopius coccus* Costa	16th
		red	carminic acid	*Dactylopius coccus* Costa	
		purple	carminic acid indigotin	*Dactylopius coccus* Costa *Indigofera tinctoria* or *Isatis tinctoria*	
		blue	indigotin	*Indigofera tinctoria* or *Isatis tinctoria*	
		yellow-1	luteolin? apigenin?	*Reseda luteola*	
		green	luteolin apigenin indigotin	*Reseda luteola* *Indigofera tinctoria* or *Isatis tinctoria*	
		yellow-2	luteolin apigenin	*Reseda luteola*	

Table 3. According to the metal threads analysis, the results of some Ottoman brocades in the Topkapi Place Museum.

Inv. No.		**Mass percentages (wt %)**									
		C	O	Mg	S	Cl	Al	Ag	Au		
13/1550	In	2,39	2,3	0,96			0,59	93,77		wide	140 micrometer
	out	2,43	1,64	1,43	1,07	3,03		90,39		thickness	5 micrometer
13/1525	In	4,76	2,13	1,05			0,97	78,00	13,09	wide	205 micrometer
	out	2,92	0,85	1,09		1,69		81,53	11,92	thickness	6 micrometer
13/1527	In	2,76		0,95				96,29		wide	276 micrometer
	out	3,13	1,41	1,07	0,69	0,67		90,94	2,09	thickness	7 micrometer
13/1539	In	13,2	4,28	0,71	0,34	7,42	0,48	73,57		wide	220 micrometer
	out	5,56	5,31	0,94	0,82	4,17	0,76	78,59	3,86	thickness	9 micrometer
13/1528	In	17,21	7,33	0,68	4,54	1,35		68,89		wide	155 micrometer
	out	3,48	2,24	0,88	3,14	2,61		87,65		thickness	9,5 micrometer